Plastic Pollution, Theological Ethics, *and the* Call of *Laudato Si'*

Edited by

Andrea Vicini, SJ,
Philip J. Landrigan,
and
Karen Bullock

◆PICKWICK *Publications* • Eugene, Oregon

PLASTIC POLLUTION, THEOLOGICAL ETHICS, AND THE CALL OF
LAUDATO SI'

Copyright © 2025 Andrea Vicini, SJ, Philip J. Landrigan, and Karen Bullock. All rights reserved. Except for brief quotations in critical publications or reviews, no part of this book may be reproduced in any manner without prior written permission from the publisher. Write: Permissions, Wipf and Stock Publishers,

199 W. 8th Ave., Suite 3, Eugene, OR 97401.

Pickwick Publications
An Imprint of Wipf and Stock Publishers
199 W. 8th Ave., Suite 3
Eugene, OR 97401

www.wipfandstock.com

SOFTCOVER ISBN: 979-8-3852-5533-7
HARDCOVER ISBN: 979-8-3852-5534-4
EBOOK ISBN: 979-8-3852-5535-1

Cataloguing-in-Publication data:

Names: Vicini, Andrea, editor. | Landrigan, Philip J., editor. | Bullock, Karen, editor.

Title: Plastic pollution, theological ethics, and the call of Laudato si' / edited by Andrea Vicini, Philip J. Landrigan, and Karen Bullock.

Description: Eugene, OR : Pickwick Publications, 2025 | Series: Global Theological Ethics

Identifiers: ISBN 979-8-3852-5533-7 (paperback) | ISBN 979-8-3852-5534-4 (hardcover) | ISBN 979-8-3852-5535-1 (ebook)

Subjects: LCSH: Catholic Church. Pope (2013–2025 : Francis). Laudato si'. | Plastics—Environmental aspects.

Classification: BX1795.H82 .P55 2025 (print) | BX1795.H82 (ebook)

DEDICATION

To all those affected by plastic pollution and to everyone committed to address the plastics crisis.

Global Theological Ethics—Book Series

Series Editors

Jason King, St. Mary's—San Antonio, TX
M. Therese Lysaught, Loyola University Chicago

The Global Theological Ethics book series focuses on works that feature authors from around the world, draw on resources from the traditions of Catholic theological ethics, and attend to concrete issues facing the world today. It advances the *Journal of Moral Theology*'s mission of fostering scholarship deeply rooted in traditions of inquiry about the moral life, engaged with contemporary issues, and exploring the interface of Catholic moral theology philosophy, economics, political philosophy, psychology, and more.

This series is sponsored in conjunction with the Catholic Theological Ethics in the World Church. CTEWC recognizes the need to dialogue from and beyond local cultures and to interconnect within a world church. Its global network of scholars, practitioners, and activists fosters cross-cultural, interdisciplinary conversations—via conferences, symposia, and colloquia, both in-person and virtually—about critical issues in theological ethics, shaped by shared visions of hope.

Online versions of the volumes in the *Global Theological Ethics* series are available for free download as chapters at jmt.scholasticahq.com. Paper copies may be purchased from Wipf & Stock. This dual approach reflects the *Journal of Moral Theology*'s commitment to the common good as it seeks to make the scholarship of Catholic theological ethicists broadly available, especially across borders. Additionally, you can find the series listed on the CTEWC website at catholicethics.com/book-series/catholic-theological-ethics-series/.

Series Titles

Ethical Challenges in Global Public Health: Climate Change, Pollution, and the Health of the Poor, edited by Philip J. Landrigan and Andrea Vicini, SJ (2021)

The Rising Global Cancer Pandemic: Health, Ethics, and Social Justice, edited by Andrea Vicini, SJ, Philip J. Landrigan, and Kurt Straif (2022)

Doing Theology and Theological Ethics in the Face of the Abuse Crisis, edited by Daniel J. Fleming, James F. Keenan, SJ, and Hans Zollner, SJ (2023)

A Prophet to the Peoples: Paul Farmer's Witness and Theological Ethics, edited by Jennie Weiss Block, M. Therese Lysaught, and Alexandre A. Martins (2023)

Haciendo Teología y Ética Teológica Frente a la Crisis de Abuso, edited by Daniel J. Fleming, James F. Keenan, SJ, and Hans Zollner, SJ (2024)

Reproduction and the Common Good: Global Perspectives from the Catholic Tradition, edited by Simeiqi He and Emily Reimer-Barry (2024)

Plastic Pollution, Theological Ethics, and the Call of Laudato Si', edited by Andrea Vicini, SJ, Philip J. Landrigan, and Karen Bullock (2025)

Table of Contents

Acknowledgments
The Editors ix

Preface
Andrea Vicini, SJ, and Philip J. Landrigan 1

Part 1: Framing the Issues

1. Need for New Strategies to Protect Human Health in the Age of Plastics
Judith Enck 10

2. Safeguarding Human Health against Plastics and Petrochemicals: A Scientific and Moral Imperative
Sarah Dunlop, Yannick Mulders, Louise Goodes, Hervé Raps, and Philip J. Landrigan 22

Part 2: Assessing the Challenges

3. The Disproportionate Impacts of Plastics on Low- and Middle-Income Countries
Adetoun Mustapha Olaitan 52

4. Plastics and Inclusive Wealth
Pushpam Kumar 59

Part 3: Responding Ethically

5. Becoming Plastic, Transforming Justice
Willis Jenkins 67

6. Plastics, Markets, and the Preferential Option for the Poor: What Can Be Done, and by Whom?
Christina G. McRorie 83

7. The Plastics Crisis and Catholic Social Teaching
Andrea Vicini, SJ 98

Part 4: Striving for Solutions

8. Advancing a Global Treaty on Plastic Pollution: Current Status and Challenges
Margaret Spring and Cindy Matuch 109

Part 5: Joining Religious Commitments

9. A Moral Roadmap for Ending the Global Plastics Crisis
The Rev. Mitchell C. Hescox 121

10. A Message from Judaism
Rabbi Leonid Feldman 140

11. A Message from the Eastern Orthodox Church
His All-Holiness Ecumenical Patriarch Bartholomew 142

12. A Message from Tibetan Buddhism
The Dalai Lama 144

Part 6: Supporting Political Engagements

13. A Message from the Prince of Monaco
Albert II 147

14. Proposing and Signing a Declaration
Karen Bullock 149

15. Declaration: Our Shared Responsibility to End Plastic Pollution, Protect Human Health, and Advance Social Justice for All
Conference Participants 152

Conclusion

16. A Manual for Moral Collectives: Our Shared Responsibility to End Plastic Pollution, Protect Human Health, and Advance Social Justice for All
James F. Keenan, SJ 158

Acknowledgments

We express our deep gratitude to our many colleagues—at Boston College, across the US, and internationally—who generously shared their passion and expertise in reflecting on the ethical challenges that characterize the plastic crisis and how it affects local and global efforts to promote health. We are grateful that some of their contributions are gathered in this book.

The Boston College community—with its dedicated faculty, students, administrators, and staff, its commitment to science and the humanities, and its longing for social justice—continues to be an inspiring formative context for ethically inspired education, research, and practice in addressing challenging issues in global public health. Boston College has enabled us to engage in examining urgent issues in global public health, identifying and addressing social inequities, striving to promote the common good, advancing justice, and caring for the Earth—our common home. These are complex times that demand determination, ingenuity, and creativity to address plastic pollution together with the many pre-existing and enduring challenges that affect the health of individuals, populations, and of the whole planet. For all these reasons, we are deeply thankful.

This volume continues to rely on and joins diverse academic entities and initiatives at Boston College that foster this ethos and aim at training students and citizens attentive to address ethically and with competence the multiple issues affecting global public health across the planet. In particular, we mention the Institute for the Liberal Arts; the School of Social Work, and particularly Dr. Summer Hawkins, who co-organized the October 2024 conference "Joining Science and Theology to End Plastic Pollution, Protect Health, and Advance Social Justice"; the Gloria L. and Charles I. Clough School of Theology and Ministry; the Schiller Institute for Integrated Science and Society; the Law School; the William F. Connell School of Nursing, with its minor and major in Global Public Health and the Common Good; and, within the Morrissey College of Arts and

Acknowledgments

Sciences: the Biology Department; the Earth and Environmental Sciences Department, with its Environmental Studies program; the Engineering Department, with its major in Human-Centered Engineering; and the minor in Medical Humanities, Health, and Culture.

Andrea Vicini, SJ, Philip J. Landrigan, and Karen Bullock

Preface

Andrea Vicini, SJ, and Philip J. Landrigan

In August 1945, with the dropping of the atomic bombs on Hiroshima and Nagasaki, the world entered a new geologic epoch, the Anthropocene. This is the first time in all of history in which human beings have become the dominant force on Earth, the shapers of the planet's environment.[1]

The environment is essential to all life on Earth, and the health of the planetary environment profoundly influences the state of human health. Human species have inhabited the earth for hundreds of thousands of years, but it is only in the past eleven thousand years, the time since the last ice age—the Holocene Epoch—that civilizations have risen, because it is only in this period that an environment favorable to human thriving has been sustained over a span of many centuries.

In the Holocene, the climate has been relatively stable, and the environment has provided clean air with sufficient oxygen, fresh water, healthy soils, and abundant food. In this epoch, humans have been able for the first time to build cities, accumulate great wealth, generate new knowledge, explore the farthest corners of the planet, write books, elucidate the mysteries of the human body, visit the bottom of the oceans, and venture into space.

These advances have greatly benefited human health and well-being, and they have led to doubling of the human life span and the conquest of many dread diseases. They have come, however, at great cost to the planet, and they have produced great inequality. They have relied on the combustion of vast quantities of fossil fuels, massive consumption of

---

[1] See Sarah Whitmee, Andy Haines, Chris Beyrer, Frederick Boltz, Anthony G. Capon, Braulio Ferreira de Souza Dias, et al., "Safeguarding Human Health in the Anthropocene Epoch: Report of the Rockefeller Foundation-Lancet Commission on Planetary Health," *Lancet* 386, no. 10007 (2015): 1973–2028.

minerals, widespread deforestation, progressively heavier applications of insecticides and herbicides, and the production and release into the environment of enormous quantities of chemicals and plastics.[2] In short, they have strip-mined the Earth's resources and mortgaged humanity's future.

The consequences are climate change, pollution, and biodiversity loss—the 'Triple Planetary Crisis.' These threats are responsible for more than nine million premature deaths each year as well as widespread disease and disability.[3] They can be directly attributed to the currently prevalent, linear, take-make-use-dispose economic paradigm—termed by Pope Francis "the throwaway culture"[4]—in which natural resources and human capital are viewed as abundant and expendable, and the consequences of their reckless exploitation are given little heed. This paradigm focuses almost exclusively on short-term economic gain, as measured by the Gross Domestic Product (GDP), while ignoring natural capital and human capital.[5] Hence, it fails to link economic development to social justice, and it is ultimately unsustainable.

Technical and legal solutions to the planetary crises of the Anthropocene are necessary and frequently effective, as seen in the sharp declines in manufacture of chlorofluorocarbons that resulted from the

---

[2] See Philip J. Landrigan, Richard Fuller, Nereus J. R. Acosta, Olusoji Adeyi, Robert Arnold, Niladri Nil Basu, et al., "The *Lancet* Commission on Pollution and Health," *Lancet* 391, no. 10119 (2018): 462–512.

[3] See Landrigan, et al., "The *Lancet* Commission on Pollution and Health."

[4] Francis, *Laudato Si': On Care for Our Common Home* (2015), www.vatican.va/content/francesco/en/encyclicals/documents/papa-francesco_20150524_enciclica-laudato-si.html, nos. 16, 22, 43.

[5] See Partha Dasgupta, Shunsuke Managi, and Pushpam Kumar, "The Inclusive Wealth Index and Sustainable Development Goals," *Sustainability Science* 17, no. 3 (2022): 899–903.

Montreal Protocol,[6] reductions in air pollution following the passage of clean air laws,[7] and recent large decreases in the costs of renewable energy.[8]

All these solutions have, however, been reactive. None offer protection against hazards yet to come. Durable protection against current and future dangers will require solutions that extend beyond specific threats and technical fixes. Such solutions must address the underlying political, economic, ethical, and moral causes of the planetary crisis.[9]

It was in this spirit that Boston College convened an international Conference, "Joining Science and Theology to End Plastic Pollution, Protect Health, and Advance Social Justice," on October 4–5, 2024. This conference combined a state-of-the-art review of current knowledge of plastics' harms to human health and the global environment[10] with an exploration of the social consequences and the ethical foundations of the plastics crisis. The goal was to bring moral clarity to the conversation on plastics. The conference brought together scientists, ethicists, lawyers, economists, engineers, policy makers, and religious leaders. It was based on the recognition that the plastics crisis is more than an environmental threat, and that like climate change, air pollution, biodiversity loss, and escalating inequality, it is also a social and ethical challenge. It is a crisis that demands solutions that are based on the best science, but that are also just and ethically sound. This volume gathers the papers presented at the conference.

---

[6] See United Nations Environment Programme (UNEP), "The Montreal Protocol on Substances That Deplete the Ozone Layer" (1989), ozone.unep.org/treaties/montreal-protocol-substances-deplete-ozone-layer/text.
[7] See Landrigan, Fuller, Acosta, et al., "The *Lancet* Commission on Pollution and Health."
[8] See Max Roser, "Why Did Renewables Become So Cheap So Fast?" (2020), ourworldindata.org/cheap-renewables-growth.
[9] See Francis, *Laudato Si'*, no. 139.
[10] See Philip J. Landrigan, Hervé Raps, Maureen Cropper, Caroline Bald, Manuel Brunner, Elvia Maya Canonizado, et al., "The Minderoo-Monaco Commission on Plastics and Human Health," *Annals of Global Health* 89, no. 1 (2023): doi.org/10.5334/aogh.4056.

Preface

Overview

To articulate a critical analysis and propose solutions, the volume frames the needed issues, assesses the challenges, responds ethically to both issues and challenges, and strives for feasible solutions. Religious commitments and political engagements further enrich the book's contributions and aim at motivating sustainable actions. The Declaration that ended the 2024 conference, entitled "Our Shared Responsibility to End Plastic Pollution, Protect Health, and Advance Social Justice for All," exemplifies this interdisciplinary approach and aims at gathering diverse moral agents who are concerned about plastic pollution and its effects on humankind and the Earth, and who long to see resolute international actions, including a global treaty on plastic production and disposal.

In the opening chapter, Judith Enck provides a broad overview of the ways that plastics increasingly affect the planet and human health. She also critically examines the failures of recycling. She urges faith communities and civil society to commit, acknowledging the gravity of plastic pollution and responding to it with urgent actions (e.g., policies and regulations), unmasking false solutions.

In Chapter Two, Sarah Dunlop, Yannick Mulders, Louise Goodes, Hervé Raps, and Philip J. Landrigan richly document the scientific and technical aspects of plastics production, recycling, and disposal, making clear the ways in which this topic is complex and ethically problematic. They stress how some types and uses of plastics are both useful and necessary (e.g., in healthcare practice), but, at the same time, plastics production, consumption, and disposal pose growing threats to human and planetary health. In compelling ways, these authors demand an ethically-grounded treaty with concrete provisions—like a global cap on plastic production and a strict regulation of plastic chemicals—that will prioritize the protection of human health, human rights, and planetary health.

In their respective chapters, Adetoun Mustapha Olaitan and Pushpam Kumar assess the ongoing challenges. First, Mustapha Olaitan highlights the disproportionate negative impacts of plastics on low- and middle-income countries, mostly in the Global South. Existing inequities that depend on the Global North and Global South divide have dire implications for women and vulnerable populations. While striving to hold plastic producers accountable, it is necessary to support community-led initiatives and education. Successful strategies must address the diverse and context-specific technological, social, political, ecological, and economic challenges that people and their communities face across the planet.

Second, Pushpam Kumar stresses how the harms caused by plastics result in increased mortality and morbidity, which in turn undermine human capital and compromise sustainable growth. However, the exclusive use of Gross Domestic Product (GDP) as a metric of national wealth fails to measure these damages. The use of the Inclusive Wealth Index to supplement the GDP could provide a more comprehensive assessment of economy-environment interactions and better assess inequities than the GDP alone and a better guide to implement ethically-grounded, health-protective, and economically-sound remedies to the global plastics crisis.

Three authors articulate ethical responses. Willis Jenkins discusses how, in early Christian thought, the word 'plastic' pointed to the human ability of being molded by divine action. Then plastic became emblematic of the human capability to pollute and of colonial powers to dominate human beings and the Earth. Jenkins argues that we should retrieve the original meaning and assume our responsibility, caring for our planet. In engaging the Minderoo-Monaco Report, he highlights six approaches that could turn plastics and their impacts into ethical problems that could be tackled: trash containment, bodily contamination, violence and injury, distributive injustice, multispecies injustice, colonial injustice, and integrative repair. The chapter ends by commenting on five tactics which could guide our actions: cap production, inclusive science, extended producer responsibility, rights of rivers and oceans, and living a good life with plastic.

Preface

Christina McRorie stresses how disproportionate harms affect the most vulnerable and call for drastic changes to our current trajectory of producing, using, and disposing of plastics. When considering these global economic factors, it is tempting to conclude that until governments step in to stop markets, we are effectively powerless. While granting the necessity of coordinated political action, McRorie proposes that economics and Catholic social thought offer resources for taking a less fatalistic approach, and viewing the economy—and thus the plastics crisis—in more three-dimensional terms. Hence, she sketches a view highlighting the deeply social nature of all economic activity and how market processes and outcomes are sustained and shaped by cultural norms and practices undertaken at all levels of society. Such a perspective broadens our sense of who participates in economic governance and of what forms of action can be taken to steer global and local economies away from our mindlessly increasing reliance on plastics, implementing the preferential option for the poor.

Andrea Vicini argues that the virtue of social trust is necessary to address the plastic pollution crisis. Moreover, other virtues—e.g., prudence, justice, and solidarity—contribute to strengthen personal and social agency and inform concrete practices. Furthermore, civil society should not presume that technology is *the* only solution to address the gravity of the global environmental crisis. Following Pope Francis's invitation to examine any "technocratic paradigm," both a critical assessment of technological developments and a strengthened social awareness may lead to promoting environmentally sustainable alternatives and embracing forms of resistance to unquestioned uses of plastic products. Finally, education and formation empower moral agents and lead to needed structural transformations and changes.

Striving for solutions, Margaret Spring and Cindy Matuch discuss the current status of an international legally-binding instrument to address plastic pollution. Their historical account considers critical areas that have been discussed among UN members and have shaped the evolution of the text which will be examined at the 2025 meeting of the Intergovernmental

Negotiating Committee. Finally, they provide a short analysis of the major areas of alignment and disjunct that arose during the last negotiating meeting, which may shape the final negotiations in 2025.

Religious voices and constituencies, with practices embraced by communities of believers, represent a major presence with global civil society. The Reverend Mitchell C. Hescox draws on his evangelical commitments, encounters, and experiences, highlighting the difficult task of raising awareness of the gravity of the climate crisis and plastic pollution. An increased awareness should lead to concrete actions aimed at protecting the environment and addressing the ongoing global plastics crisis. To foster awareness and support actions, Hescox interprets key Scriptural passages, articulates the evangelical commitment to protect life, and integrates contributions which depend on his training in Family Systems Theory. The outcome is a moral roadmap for responding to the global plastics crisis and, hopefully, ending it.

Other religious voices further contribute to strengthen religious commitments. Rabbi Leonid Feldman stresses the urgency of repairing our world—Tikkun Olam—because of our responsibility to work towards healing the environment and be good stewards of God's creation. His All-Holiness Ecumenical Patriarch Bartholomew invites us to recognize the invaluable gift of creation, being grateful for such a gift, and to hand it down to future generations. Finally, His Holiness the Dalai Lama exhorts us to embrace our universal responsibility and care for the Earth.

To support political action, the Prince of Monaco invites us to join his commitment and engagement, striving to address the global crisis of plastic pollution. Karen Bullock highlights the rationale informing the Declaration "Our Shared Responsibility to End Plastic Pollution, Protect Human Health, and Advance Social Justice for All," which urges UN negotiators to incorporate provisions into the Treaty aimed at advancing human rights and protecting the vulnerable and the planet against plastic's threats to human and planetary health. Finally, the Declaration highlights the findings that surfaced during the 2024 conference and makes a series of recommendations. To effectively confront the global plastics crisis, legal and technical solutions, such as the UN Global Plastics Treaty, should be developed and implemented. At the same time, it is necessary to reexamine our relationships with each other and with the Earth. We are all interconnected. Governments, international organizations, corporations, and every citizen share the responsibility to be good stewards of God's creation and critically examine lifestyles and the use of Earth's resources.

To conclude, James F. Keenan, SJ, provides a critical reading of the book. He describes the volume as a manual which voices the concerns of collectives and reaches out to collectives. For Keenan, this book exemplifies our shared responsibility to care for our common home and allows moral agents and civil society to advocate for concrete actions that should lead us to end plastic pollution, protect health, and advance social justice for all human beings while benefiting our planet.

The task of ending plastic pollution might appear unrealistic to some and daunting to others. Our hope is that this book will join many other efforts and collaborative actions—scientific, ethical, religious, and social—which strive to address the plastic pollution crisis and succeed in protecting humankind and the Earth, addressing social and environmental inequities, and entrusting a more just and healthier planet to our current and future generations.

Part 1

Framing *the* Issues

1. The Need for New Strategies to Protect Human Health in the Age of Plastics

Judith Enck

Thousands of years ago, Rabbi Tarfon (70–135 C.E.) prophetically said, "Do not be daunted by the enormity of the world's grief. Do justly now, walk humbly now. You are not obligated to complete the work, but neither are you free to abandon it." These inspired words apply to the current plastics crisis.

Humanity has exceeded a tipping point in the production of plastics, and global plastic production continues to rise at an alarming rate.[1] Micro- and nanoparticles from plastic waste have now been found in every corner of the planet from the Mariana Trench to Mount Everest.[2] Plastic has infiltrated our food, our water, our air, our soil, and our bodies.[3] It contributes to climate change at every stage of its life cycle.[4] Indeed, there is nowhere on Earth to escape the presence of toxic plastic pollution. The time is now for faith communities, the public, and policymakers to come together to address the urgency of plastic pollution.

---

[1] See Alden Wicker, "The Plastics Crisis Is Now a Global Human Health Crisis, Experts Say," *Mongabay*, November 19, 2024, news.mongabay.com/2024/11/the-plastics-crisis-is-now-a-global-human-health-crisis-experts-say/.

[2] See Sanae Chiba, Hideaki Saito, Ruth Fletcher, Takayuki Yogi, Makino Kayo, Shin Miyagi, et al., "Human Footprint in the Abyss: 30 Year Records of Deep-sea Plastic Debris," *Marine Policy* 96 (2018): 204–212; Imogen E. Napper, Bede F.R. Davies, Heather Clifford, Sandra Elvin, Heather J. Koldewey, Paul A. Mayewski, et al., "Reaching New Heights in Plastic Pollution: Preliminary Findings of Microplastics on Mount Everest," *One Earth* 3, no. 5 (2020): 621–630.

[3] See Center for International Environmental Law, *Plastic & Health: The Hidden Costs of a Plastic Planet*, ed. A. Kistler (2019), www.ciel.org/plasticandhealth.

[4] See Center for International Environmental Law, *Plastic & Health*.

A Need for New Strategies

In November 2023, the United Nations Climate Change Conference, COP28, hosted its first-ever Faith Pavilion, signifying a recognition of the role of faith communities as partners in fighting global climate change. Faith communities represent access to "millions of acres, billions of people, and trillions of dollars," said the organizers. Indeed, faith-based organizations own eight percent of all habitable land surface, fifty percent of schools worldwide, and make up over thirty-five percent of the global fossil fuel divestment movement, which has mobilized more than $40 trillion in commitments.[5] Powerful declarations, such as Pope Francis' 2015 encyclical letter *Laudato Si'*[6] and the 2024 Muslim Al-Mizan statement,[7] represent pinnacle achievements in faith contributions to the climate movement, inspiring awe and reverence for nature, speaking the truth of the existential threat of climate change, and imploring humanity to change course.

Perhaps most importantly, faith communities use their moral authority to name the damage of ecological destruction, draw upon the spiritual resources of their respective traditions to work through ecological grief, activate people to look inward and adopt sustainable practices, and mobilize their communities to advocate for policy that can affect institutional change.

The movement to address plastic pollution is often siloed outside the climate movement. But plastics are made from chemicals and fossil fuels, and if plastic were a country, it would be the fifth largest source of greenhouse gas emissions behind only China, the United States, India, and Russia.[8] While faith engagement with the plastic issue has not yet reached

---

[5] See Global Fossil Fuel Divestment Commitments Database, divestmentdatabase.org/.
[6] See Francis, *Laudato Si': On Care for Our Common Home* (2015), www.vatican.va/content/francesco/en/encyclicals/documents/papa-francesco_20150524_enciclica-laudato-si.html.
[7] See Othman Llewellyn, Fazlun Khalid, Aishah Ali Abdallah, Ibrahim Özdemir, Evren Tok, Fachruddin M. Mangunjaya, et al., *Al-Mizan: Covenant for the Earth* (The Islamic Foundation for Ecology and Environmental Sciences, 2024).
[8] See Matt Simon, *A Poison like No Other: How Microplastics Corrupted Our Planet and Our Bodies* (Island Press, 2022), 252.

the level of that of the climate crisis, the necessity for a moral framework on plastics is just as urgent.

Faith communities employ an alternative epistemology and modality in their orientation to these crises that can illuminate the moral imperative to take action. As former UN Development Program Administrator James Gustave Speth once noted: "I used to think that top environmental problems were biodiversity loss, ecosystem collapse, and climate change. I thought that thirty years of good science could address these problems. I was wrong. The top environmental problems are selfishness, greed, and apathy, and to deal with these we need a cultural and spiritual transformation."[9]

In 2019, the United Nations Environment Programme's Faith Working Group on Pollution adopted its resolution "Stop Plastic Pollution and Restore Our World," calling for—among other provisions—plastic-reduction policies, bans on the use of certain single-use plastics, strategies leveraging faith-based platforms to raise awareness of plastic pollution, and government accountability for the unequal effects that plastic has on marginalized and vulnerable societies.[10] Since the 2022 adoption of the UN Environment Assembly resolution to address plastic pollution, a growing number of faith-based organizations from a wide range of religious and spiritual traditions have participated in the Intergovernmental Negotiating Committee on Plastic Pollution (INC) meetings. Some of these initiatives are specifically targeting pollution at the community level while others focus on the rights of key communities impacted.

---

[9] Quoted in: Geoff Davies, "COP28: Humans of All Faiths (and No Faith) Have a Limited Window of Opportunity to Act on the Climate Crisis," *Daily Maverick* (November 30, 2023), www.dailymaverick.co.za/opinionista/2023-11-30-cop28-humans-of-all-faiths-and-no-faith-have-a-limited-window-of-opportunity-to-act-on-the-climate-crisis/.

[10] See United Nations Environment Programme (UNEP), "Stop Plastic Pollution and Restore Our World," March 2022 (updated: July 2024), drive.google.com/file/d/1QhZFTXveeqG1n-rP2yWDk4n0x0T6dtX9/view.

A Need for New Strategies

All the world's religions share a commitment to truth, both the spiritual and moral truths upheld by our traditions as well as by an honest appraisal of the reality of the world in which we live. The Swiss Reformed Christian theologian Karl Barth (1886–1968) once said, "Take your Bible and take your newspaper, and read both. But interpret newspapers from your Bible."[11] While *interpretation* of the reality of the world's plastic pollution crisis will depend on each faith tradition's customs, practices, and beliefs, the facts on the ground remain the same. However, when these interpretive perspectives are held together, each tradition speaking from its own deeply held faith, we can build a powerful moral and spiritual framework and mandate for the movement to end plastic pollution.

The first step along this journey is acknowledging the truth: plastic is a threat to the environment, the climate, human health, and environmental justice.

Plastic Pollution in the Environment

Thirty-three billion pounds of plastic end up in our oceans each year—mostly from land—and much of that is unnecessary, single-use plastic that we could easily do without.[12] In fact, the top ten most common waste items found in worldwide coastal cleanups in 2024 were single-use plastic products, including beverage bottles, food wrappers, bags, food containers, cups, plates, straws, and stirrers.[13] This plastic persists in the environment at least for decades, choking marine life, and entering our food, soil, air, and water. Marine, freshwater, and terrestrial animals consume and become

---

[11] "Barth in Retirement," *Time*, May 13, 1963, time.com/archive/6831843/barth-in-retirement/.

[12] See Andrew Forrest, Luca Giacovazzi, Sarah Dunlop, Julia Reisser, David Tickler, Alan Jamieson, and Jessica J. Meeuwig, "Eliminating Plastic Pollution: How a Voluntary Contribution from Industry Will Drive the Circular Plastics Economy," *Frontiers in Marine Science* 6 (September 24, 2019), doi.org/10.3389/fmars.2019.00627.

[13] See Ocean Conservancy, "Cleanup Reports: International Coastal Cleanup," September 4, 2024, oceanconservancy.org/trash-free-seas/international-coastal-cleanup/annual-data-release/.

entangled in plastic trash, threatening their ability to eat, function, and survive.[14] Seabirds mistake red or orange plastic for shrimp. Sea turtles mistake plastic bags for delicious jellyfish. The planet's creatures have a diet filled with microplastics, which comes with a whole host of chemicals, many of which are toxic.[15]

Plastics and Human Health

With plastic production expected to triple by 2060, this problem will only get worse.[16] And animals are not the only ones with a plastic-filled diet. The presence of microplastics contaminates the planet we depend on for survival and ultimately lodge themselves in the human body—from our hearts,[17] lungs,[18]

---

[14] See Chris Wilcox, Melody Puckridge, Qamar A Schuyler, Kathy Townsend, and Britta Denise Hardesty, "A Quantitative Analysis Linking Sea Turtle Mortality and Plastic Debris Ingestion," *Scientific Reports* 8, no. 1 (August 16, 2018), doi.org/10.1038/s41598-018-30038-z.

[15] See Meysam Saeedi, "How Microplastics Interact with Food Chain: A Short Overview of Fate and Impacts," *Journal of Food Science and Technology* 61, no. 3 (2024): 403–413.

[16] See Organisation for Economic Co-operation and Development (OECD), "Global Plastic Waste Set to Almost Triple by 2060, Says OECD," Press release, June 3, 2022, www.oecd.org/en/about/news/press-releases/2022/06/global-plastic-waste-set-to-almost-triple-by-2060.html.

[17] See Julie Corliss, "Microplastics in Arteries Linked to Heart Disease Risk," *Harvard Health* (June 1, 2024), www.health.harvard.edu/heart-health/microplastics-in-arteries-linked-to-heart-disease-risk.

[18] See Lauren C. Jenner, Jeanette M. Rotchell, Robert T. Bennett, Michael Cowen, Vasileios Tentzeris, and Laura R. Sadofsky, "Detection of Microplastics in Human Lung Tissue using μFTIR Spectroscopy," *Science of the Total Environment* 831 (July 20, 2022): 154907, doi.org/10.1016/j.scitotenv.2022.154907.

brains,[19] and liver[20] to the placenta,[21] breast milk,[22] and even newborn babies.[23] This illustrates in the most tangible way possible what Chief Seattle so prophetically warned, that "What we do to our earth, we do to ourselves."[24]

Micro- and nanoplastic particles, which leach and shed from plastic products, contain many of the sixteen thousand chemical additives found in plastics.[25] At least 4,200 of those additives are considered to be "highly hazardous" to human health and the environment. Thousands more have not even been tested for their safety.[26] As we absorb plastics through our skin, swallow them, and breathe them, chemicals come along for the ride.[27] Chemicals found in plastics have been associated with cancer, nervous

---

[19] See Luís Fernando Amato-Lourenço, Katia Cristina Dantas, Gabriel Ribeiro Júnior, Vitor Ribeiro Paes, Rômulo Augusto Ando, Raul De Oliveira Freitas, et al., "Microplastics in the Olfactory Bulb of the Human Brain," *JAMA Network Open* 7, no. 9 (September 16, 2024): e2440018, doi.org/10.1001/jamane tworkopen.2024.40018.

[20] See Thomas Horvatits, Matthias Tamminga, Bebei Liu, Marcial Sebode, Antonella Carambia, Lutz Fischer, et al., "Microplastics Detected in Cirrhotic Liver Tissue," *Lancet* 82 (August 2022): 104147, www.thelancet.com/journals/ebiom/article/PIIS2352-3964(22)00328-0/fulltext.

[21] See Shaojie Liu, Jialin Guo, Xinyuan Liu, Ruoru Yang, Hangwei Wang, Yongyun Sun, et al., "Detection of Various Microplastics in Placentas, Meconium, Infant Feces, Breastmilk and Infant Formula: A Pilot Prospective Study," *Science of the Total Environment* 854 (September 13, 2022): 158699, doi.org/10.101 6/j.scitotenv.2022.158699.

[22] See Antonio Ragusa, Valentina Notarstefano, Alessandro Svelato, Alessia Belloni, Giorgia Gioacchini, Christine Blondeel, et al., "Raman Microspectroscopy Detection and Characterisation of Microplastics in Human Breastmilk," *Polymers* 14, no. 13 (June 30, 2022): 2700, doi.org/10.3390/polym14132700.

[23] See Antonio Ragusa, Alessandro Svelato, Criselda Santacroce, Piera Catalano, Valentina Notarstefano, Oliana Carnevali, et al., "Plasticenta: First Evidence of Microplastics in Human Placenta," *Environment International* 146 (January 2021): 106274, doi.org/10.1016/j.envint. 2020.106274.

[24] Clay Haswell, "'What We Do to Earth, We Do to Ourselves,'" *HuffPost*, April 22, 2016, huffpost.com/entry/what-we-do-to-earth-we-do_b_9751760.

[25] See Plastic Pollution Coalition, "PlastChem: State of the Science on Plastic Chemicals," March 20, 2024, www.plasticpollutioncoalition.org/resource-library/plastchem-state-of-the-science-on-plastic-chemicals.

[26] Plastic Pollution Coalition, "PlastChem: State of the Science on Plastic Chemicals."

[27] See Center for International Environmental Law, *Plastic & Health: The Hidden Costs of a Plastic Planet*.

system damage, hormone disruption, and reduced fertility.[28] In 2024, researchers found tiny plastic particles in human arteries—specifically the carotid arteries, which supply blood to the brain.[29] In this study, patients with plastic-tainted arteries were 4.5 times more likely to suffer from a cardiovascular event like heart attack or stroke.

Plastic's Climate Impacts

What many people do not realize is that the plastic pollution crisis and the climate crisis are intrinsically linked, making it impossible to fight one problem without considering the other. Plastic contributes four times more climate-forcing greenhouse gas emissions to the atmosphere each year than the global aviation industry, according to a United States federal government study released in April 2024.[30] A Beyond Plastics report found that plastic is the new coal. In the US, plastic is set to outpace coal's greenhouse gas emissions by 2030.[31]

Plastic drives climate change because plastic is made from fossil fuels and because plastic production is highly energy-intensive. Plastic contributes to climate change from the beginning of its life cycle to the end, from the greenhouse gases that escape during the extraction and refining of fossil fuels, to the energy-intensive process used to make plastic, to the emissions in its transport, and on to the greenhouse gas burden of

---

[28] See United Nations Environment Programme (UNEP), *Chemicals in Plastics: A Technical Report*, May 3, 2023, www.unep.org/resources/report/chemicals-plastics-technical-report.

[29] See Raffaele Marfella, Francesco Prattichizzo, Celestino Sardu, Gianluca Fulgenzi, Laura Graciotti, Tatiana Spadoni, et al., "Microplastics and Nanoplastics in Atheromas and Cardiovascular Events," *New England Journal of Medicine* 390, no. 10 (March 6, 2024): 900–910.

[30] See Nihan Karali, Nina Khanna, and Nihar Shah, "Climate Impact of Primary Plastic Production," *Energy Analysis & Environmental Impact Division*, April 2024, energyanalysis.lbl.gov/publications/climate-impact-primary-plastic.

[31] See Beyond Plastics, "The New Coal: Plastics and Climate Change," October 2021, www.beyondplastics.org/publications/the-new-coal.

waste management from landfilling, incineration, and recycling.[32] If we want to tackle climate change, we are going to have to tackle plastic pollution. They are one and the same.

Plastic's Impacts on Environmental Justice

Our current moment in the plastic pollution crisis demands that humanity remember its connection to Earth and other humans. The view that each person is an island, the master of their own domain and destiny must be called out for what it is—a fallacy that fails to acknowledge our dependence on this planet and our bonds with humanity.

Plastic pollution disproportionately affects low-income and vulnerable communities domestically and around the globe.[33] Communities in developing nations are plagued by rivers and beaches filled with plastic waste. Children in countries affected by waste exports should not have to spend their days sorting through plastics to earn pennies for their families. In these places around the globe, the incineration of plastics, both in households as a cheap source of fuel or at the industrial level, emits volatile organic compounds and toxins, causing serious health concerns.

Heavily polluting plastic production that affects the health of communities surrounding production facilities is surging. It is time to recognize and act on the knowledge that there is no just destination for a toxic product that originates from fossil fuels and is produced in facilities

---

[32] See Center for International Environmental Law, *Plastic & Climate: The Hidden Costs of a Plastic Planet*.

[33] See Shriver Center on Poverty Law, Emily Coffey, Kate Walz, Debbie Chizewer, Emily A. Benfer, Mark N. Templeton, and Robert Weinstock, "Poisonous Homes: The Fight for Environmental Justice in Federally Assisted Housing," Shriver Center on Poverty Law, June 2020, www.povertylaw.org/wp-content/uploads/2020/06/environmental_justice_report_final-rev2.pdf; United States Environmental Protection Agency, "Summary of Executive Order 12898: Federal Actions to Address Environmental Justice in Minority Populations and Low-Income Populations," 59 FR 7629, February 16, 1994, 19january2017snapshot.epa.gov/laws-regulations/summary-executive-order-12898-federal-actions-address-environmental-justice_.html.

that cause disease and ecological damage in the communities in which they are situated.

False Solutions

To solve the plastic pollution crisis, we must confront the problem at its source. We must address current endless and mindless increases in plastic production. Companies need to reduce the amount of plastic they produce and use. Focusing on downstream, end-use "solutions" will not bring about much needed change, despite what the plastics and petrochemical industries would have us believe. Plastics recycling has been an abysmal failure riddled with deception from its inception to today.[34]

Today in the United States, less than six percent of plastic is recycled.[35] The rest is landfilled, incinerated, or ends up in the environment. Plastics recycling was not designed to fix the problem; it was designed to make us feel better about our heavy use of plastic. As noted earlier, there are sixteen thousand different chemicals in plastic;[36] there are also many different colors and many different plastic polymers. The various plastic combinations of these chemicals, colors, and polymers can all be put in your recycling bin, but they cannot be recycled together. The countless combinations of chemicals, polymers, and colors in every county and city make the sorting and recycling process financially untenable and technically unviable. The plastics industry has known this for years but decided to mislead the public. ExxonMobil is now facing a major lawsuit from the California Attorney General Rob Bonta for misleading the

---

[34] See Beyond Plastics, "The Real Truth About the U.S. Plastics Recycling Rate," Beyond Plastics, May 2022. www.beyondplastics.org/publications/us-plastics-recycling-rate; Frontline PBS, "Plastic Wars," April 15, 2021, www.pbs.org/wgbh/frontline/documentary/plastic-wars/transcript/.
[35] See Beyond Plastics, "The Real Truth About the U.S. Plastics Recycling Rate."
[36] See Plastic Pollution Coalition, "PlastChem: State of the Science on Plastic Chemicals."

public about plastics recycling and their latest ploy, so-called chemical recycling.[37]

Chemical recycling, or what the plastics industry likes to call "advanced recycling," is just as much of a ruse.[38] It refers to largely unproven processes that use heat and/or chemicals to turn plastic waste into fossil fuels and other feedstocks to produce new plastic products. Chemical recycling is not new—it has been around, and failing, for decades. It also comes with a host of hazardous waste, air emissions, and safety issues that disproportionately affect the low-income communities and communities of color in which chemical recycling facilities are often located. Just like traditional recycling, this new form of waste management provides a distraction while companies exponentially increase the amount of plastic they flood into the world.

Real Solutions

Think of plastic recycling like this: If you walked into your bathroom to find the faucet on and water overflowing the tub, covering the floor, what is the first thing you would do? You would not start mopping, right? You would first turn off the tap. Recycling is like mopping while the tap is still on—it makes no sense. We need to turn off the tap—in other words, companies must stop producing so much plastic. Companies will not do this on their own. We need new laws, and strong enforcement of these laws, to turn off the plastics tap.

New policy is required to make this happen, because companies have proven time and time again that they are not going to do this on their own.[39] Policymakers must adopt policies on all levels of government to

---

[37] See Lisa Song, "ExxonMobil Accused of 'Deceptively' Promoting Chemical Recycling as a Solution for the Plastics Crisis," *ProPublica*, September 27, 2024, www.propublica.org/article/exxonmobil-plastics-recycling-pyrolysis-lawsuit-california.

[38] Beyond Plastics, "Chemical Recycling: A Dangerous Deception (Report)," Beyond Plastics, October 2023. www.beyondplastics.org/publications/chemical-recycling.

[39] See Beyond Plastics, "Legislation," Beyond Plastics, www.beyondplastics.org/legislation.

reduce the amount of plastic being produced and used, and incentivize the use of reuse and refill systems that provide a safer and more sustainable solution for our planet and humanity. Forty-four percent of all plastics produced are single-use.[40] While the production of plastics for any purpose is damaging to the environment and human health, targeting single-use plastics—products that are often unnecessary—makes sense.

By acknowledging the truth of humanity's problematic reliance on plastic, people of faith and conscience are moved to align their actions with their understanding. As you learn more through this book, we encourage you to share your statements of solidarity with the movement to end plastic pollution. From preaching, liturgy, ritual, prayer, music, dance, all forms of artistic expression, signage, demonstrations, newsletter articles, social media, ads in your local paper or television, etc., there are infinite ways to share the news from your unique voice and perspective.

This is a global problem that requires everyone's assistance—policymakers, businesses, and individuals of all faiths. By accepting the truth, we can move forward with real, meaningful action. There is no time to waste.

Judith Enck is President of Beyond Plastics, which she founded in 2019 to end plastic pollution through education, advocacy, and institutional change. Passionate about protecting public health and the environment, she is also Professor at Bennington College. Enck has held top influential positions in state and federal government. Appointed by President Obama, she served as the Regional Administrator of the Environmental Protection Agency, overseeing environmental protection in New York, New Jersey, eight Indian Nations, Puerto Rico and the US Virgin Islands.

---

[40] See Roland Geyer, Jenna R. Jambeck, and Kara Lavender Law, "Production, Use, and Fate of All Plastics Ever Made," *Science Advances* 3, no. 7 (July 7, 2017), doi.org/10.1126/sciadv.1700782.

Previously, Enck served as Deputy Secretary for the Environment in the New York Governor's Office, and Policy Advisor to the New York State Attorney General. She was Senior Environmental Associate with the New York Public Interest Research Group, served as Executive Director for Environmental Advocates of New York and is a past President of Hudson River Sloop Clearwater. Enck is also a panelist on a public affairs radio show on a local NPR station, WAMC, in Albany, NY.

2. Safeguarding Human Health Against Plastics and Petrochemicals: A Scientific and Moral Imperative

Sarah Dunlop, Yannick Mulders, Louise Goodes, Hervé Raps, and Philip J. Landrigan

Plastics are the signature material of our age. They have supported extraordinary advances in virtually every area of human endeavor, and they have made our daily lives very convenient. However, it is now clear that plastics are neither as safe nor as inexpensive as they seem. Plastics' benefits come at great and increasingly visible costs to human health, the environment and social justice.[1]

Plastics cause disease, disability, and premature death at every stage of their cycle—from extraction of the crude oil, fracked gas, and coal that are their main feedstocks, through transport, manufacture, use, recycling, and on to disposal into the environment as plastic waste. These harms are not equitably distributed. They fall disproportionately on the poor, minorities, and the marginalized. Groups at particularly high risk are fossil fuel extraction workers; chemical and plastic production workers; informal waste and recovery workers; persons living near fracking wells, pipelines, rail lines and compressor stations; people living in "fenceline" communities adjacent to plastic production facilities; Indigenous communities; and people in the Global South. Children and pregnant women are at especially high risk. These groups did not create the plastics crisis. They do not profit from it. They lack the power to address it. Yet they suffer its most severe consequences. They are victims of social and environmental injustice on a planetary scale.

---

[1] Philip J. Landrigan, Hervé Raps, Maureen Cropper, Caroline Bald, Manuel Brunner, Elvia Maya Canonizado, et al., "The Minderoo-Monaco Commission on Plastics and Human Health," *Annals of Global Health* 89, no. 1 (2023): doi.org/10.5334/aogh.4056.

Because plastics harm human health across their life cycle, especially among vulnerable populations, magnify social and environmental injustices, and violate human rights, the global plastics crisis is more than an environmental challenge. Like climate change, air pollution, biodiversity loss, and escalating inequality, the plastics crisis is also a social and ethical challenge.[2] It is another example of humanity's reckless strip-mining of the earth's resources and mortgaging of humanity's future for short-term economic gain.[3]

To examine the global plastics crisis through the dual perspectives of science and ethics and bring moral clarity to the conversation on control of plastics' harms, Boston College convened an international conference, "Joining Science and Theology to End Plastic Pollution, Protect Health, and Advance Social Justice," on October 4–5, 2024.[4] This chapter, based on presentations made by the authors at the conference, summarizes current information on plastics' harms to human health, the environment and the economy, drawing heavily on the findings and conclusions of the Minderoo-Monaco Commission on Plastics and Human Health.[5] Moreover, this chapter notes the disproportionate impacts of these harms on the poor and the vulnerable. It also offers some preliminary thoughts on strategies for joining science with moral theology to create ethically-

---

[2] Francis, *Laudato Si': On Care for Our Common Home* (2015), www.vatican.va/content/francesco/en/encyclicals/documents/papa-francesco_20150524_enciclica-laudato-si.html.

[3] Sarah Whitmee, Andy Haines, Chris Beyrer, Frederick Boltz, Anthony G. Capon, Braulio Ferreira de Souza Dias, et al., "Safeguarding Human Health in the Anthropocene Epoch: Report of the Rockefeller Foundation-Lancet Commission on Planetary Health," *Lancet* 386, no. 10007 (2015): 1973–2028.

[4] Boston College, "Joining Science and Theology to End Plastic Pollution, Protect Health, and Advance Social Justice" (2024), www.bc.edu/content/bc-web/academics/sites/ila/events/Plastic-Pollution-conference.html#tab-about_the_conference.

[5] Landrigan, et al., "The Minderoo-Monaco Commission on Plastics and Human Health."

sound solutions to the plastics crisis and the other great planetary challenges of our age.[6]

Human Health Impacts of Plastic Production

Global Health Impacts

Plastics are complex manufactured chemical materials. They are composed of a carbon-based polymer matrix plus more than sixteen thousand chemical additives.[7] Almost ninety-nine percent of plastic polymers and additives are made from fossil fuels—oil, gas, and coal.[8]

Plastic production is highly energy-intensive, and virtually all of the energy required for plastic manufacture comes from fossil fuel combustion.[9] The resulting greenhouse gas emissions accounted for an estimated four percent of global emissions in 2020.[10] While the production phase of plastic is the main source of greenhouse gas emissions, end-of-life

---

[6] Philip J. Landrigan, Jacqui Remond, Paolo Gomarasca, Thomas C. Chiles, Ella M. Whitman, and Lilian Ferrer, "*Laudato Si'* and the Emerging Contribution of Catholic Research Universities to Planetary Health," *Lancet Planetary Health* 8, no. 3 (2024): e140–e141, doi.org/10.1016/S2542-5196(24)00012-3.

[7] Delilah Lithner, Åke Larsson, and Göran Dave, "Environmental and Health Hazard Ranking and Assessment of Plastic Polymers Based on Chemical Composition," *Science of the Total Environment* 409, no. 18 (2011): 3309–3324.

[8] Center for International Environmental Law (CIEL), "Fueling Plastics: Fossils, Plastics, and Petrochemical Feedstocks," (2017), www.ciel.org/wp-content/uploads/2017/09/Fueling-Plastics-Fossils-Plastics-Petrochemical-Feedstocks.pdf; Almut Reichel, Xenia Trier, Ricardo Fernandez, Ioannis Bakas, and Bastian Zeiger, *Plastics, the Circular Economy and Europe's Environment: A Priority for Action* (European Environment Agency, 2021).

[9] Livia Cabernard, Stephan Pfister, Christopher Oberschelp, and Stefanie Hellweg, "Growing Environmental Footprint of Plastics Driven by Coal Combustion," *Nature Sustainability* 5, no. 2 (2022): 139–148.

[10] International Energy Agency, "Global Energy Review 2021: Assessing the Effects of Economic Recoveries on Global Energy Demand and Co2 Emissions in 2021" (2021), www.iea.org/reports/global-energy-review-2021.

phase emissions associated with plastic waste burning also contribute, accounting for nearly ten percent of total emissions.[11] Today's enormous and ever-increasing production, use and disposal into the environment of virgin plastics (504 Mt [milli] in 2022) and other petrochemicals threatens the safe operating space for humanity.[12] Single-use plastic packaging, especially food packaging, is the largest contributor to plastic waste.

Local Health Impacts

Plastic production creates extensive hazards for human health and the environment, with fossil fuel extraction, plastic production workers, plastic waste pickers, and residents of vulnerable "fenceline" communities living closely adjacent to production facilities suffering the most.[13]

Fossil Fuel Extraction: Particulate Matter Pollution

Extraction of oil, gas, and coal for plastic manufacture produces extensive airborne particulate matter (PM) pollution, which arises from mining, drilling, transport, wells and flaring.[14] Exposure to airborne PM pollution contributes to disease and premature death in workers and nearby fenceline communities. Fine PM can penetrate deep into the lungs, increasing risk in adults for cardiovascular disease, stroke, chronic

---

[11] Jiajia Zheng and Sangwon Suh, "Strategies to Reduce the Global Carbon Footprint of Plastics," *Nature Climate Change* 9, no. 5 (2019): 374–378, doi.org/10.1038/s41558-019-0459-z.

[12] Patricia Villarrubia-Gómez, Bethanie Carney Almroth, Marcus Eriksen, Morten Ryberg, and Sarah E. Cornell, "Plastics Pollution Exacerbates the Impacts of All Planetary Boundaries," *One Earth* 7, no. 12 (2024): 2119–2138.

[13] Jason D. Rivera and Steve Lerner, "Sacrifice Zones: The Front Lines of Toxic Chemical Exposure in the United States," *Community Development* 52, no. 5 (2021): 630–631.

[14] Dara O'Rourke and Sarah Connolly, "Just Oil? The Distribution of Environmental and Social Impacts of Oil Production and Consumption," *Annual Review of Environment and Resources* 28 (2003): 587–617.

obstructive pulmonary disease, lung cancer and diabetes,[15] as well as dementia,[16] and in infants and children increasing risk for premature birth and low birth weight (which themselves are risk factors for chronic diseases in adult life), stillbirth,[17] impaired lung development and asthma,[18] as well as IQ loss, memory deficits, behavioural dysfunction, reductions in brain volume, and increased risks of attention deficit hyperactivity disorder (ADHD) and autism spectrum disorder (ASD).[19] Coal dust inhalation results in further specific health impacts in miners, including pneumoconiosis, silicosis and emphysema[20] and in increasing respiratory infections for exposed nearby communities.[21]

Fossil Fuel Extraction: Ozone Pollution and Other Pollutant Emissions

---

[15] GBD Risk Factors Collaborators, "Global Burden of 87 Risk Factors in 204 Countries and Territories, 1990–2019: A Systematic Analysis for the Global Burden of Disease Study 2019," *Lancet* 396, no. 10258 (2020): 1223–1249.

[16] Eirini Dimakakou, Helinor J. Johnston, George Streftaris, and John W. Cherrie, "Exposure to Environmental and Occupational Particulate Air Pollution as a Potential Contributor to Neurodegeneration and Diabetes: A Systematic Review of Epidemiological Research," *International Journal of Environmental Research and Public Health* 15, no. 8 (2018), doi.org/10.3390/ijerph15081704.

[17] Bruce Bekkar, Susan Pacheco, Rupa Basu, and Nathaniel DeNicola, "Association of Air Pollution and Heat Exposure with Preterm Birth, Low Birth Weight, and Stillbirth in the US: A Systematic Review," *JAMA Netw Open* 3, no. 6 (2020): e208243, doi.org/10.1001/jamanetworkopen.2020.8243.

[18] Molini M. Patel and Rachel L. Miller, "Air Pollution and Childhood Asthma: Recent Advances and Future Directions," *Current Opinion in Pediatrics* 21, no. 2 (2009): 235–242.

[19] Heather E. Volk, Frederica Perera, Joseph M. Braun, et al., "Prenatal Air Pollution Exposure and Neurodevelopment: A Review and Blueprint for a Harmonized Approach Within Echo," *Environmental Research* 196 (2021): 110320, doi.org/10.1016/j.envres.2020.110320.

[20] Long Fan and Shimin M. Liu, "Respirable Nano-Particulate Generations and Their Pathogenesis in Mining Workplaces: A Review," *International Journal of Coal Science & Technology* 8, no. 2 (2021): 179–198.

[21] Juciano Gasparotto and Kátia Da Boit Martinello, "Coal as an Energy Source and Its Impacts on Human Health," *Energy Geoscience* 2, no. 2 (2021): 113–120.

Ground-level ozone is formed in the air surrounding gas and oil extraction sites.[22] It is a respiratory irritant that is especially dangerous for children and the elderly. Exposure can lead to asthma and chronic obstructive pulmonary disease.[23]

Fossil Fuel Extraction: Other Pollutant Emissions

Conventional oil, gas and coal extraction, and unconventional extraction of oil and gas—i.e., fracking—expose "fenceline" communities and workers to multiple hazardous emissions including gases (e.g., methane, carbon monoxide, sulphur dioxide), heavy metals such as mercury, solvents (benzene, xylene, toluene) and other volatile organic compounds (VOCs).[24] A range of health impacts are linked to these exposures. For example, some VOCs can cause damage to the liver, kidneys, and central nervous system,[25] others increase risk of neuropathy and asthma,[26] while

---

[22] Christopher S. Malley, Daven K. Henze, Johan C. I. Kuylenstierna, Harry W. Vallack, Yanko Davila, Susan C. Anenberg, et al., "Updated Global Estimates of Respiratory Mortality in Adults >/=30years of Age Attributable to Long-Term Ozone Exposure," *Environmental Health Perspectives* 125, no. 8 (2017): 087021, doi.org/10.1289/EHP1390.

[23] Theo Colborn, Kim Schultz, Lucille Herrick, and Carol Kwiatkowski, "An Exploratory Study of Air Quality near Natural Gas Operations," *Human and Ecological Risk Assessment* 20, no. 1 (2014): 86–105.

[24] Landrigan, et al., "The Minderoo-Monaco Commission on Plastics and Human Health."

[25] Wen-Tien Tsai, "An Overview of Health Hazards of Volatile Organic Compounds Regulated as Indoor Air Pollutants," *Reviews on Environmental Health* 34, no. 1 (2019): 81–89.

[26] Diane A. Garcia-Gonzales, Seth B. C. Shonkoff, Jake Hays, and Michael Jerrett, "Hazardous Air Pollutants Associated with Upstream Oil and Natural Gas Development: A Critical Synthesis of Current Peer-Reviewed Literature," *Annual Revue of Public Health* 40 (2019): 283–304; Mary D. Willis, Todd A. Jusko, Jill S. Halterman, and Elaine L. Hill, "Unconventional Natural Gas Development and Pediatric Asthma Hospitalizations in Pennsylvania," *Environmental Research* 166 (2018): 402–408.

still others are known carcinogens, such as benzene, 1,3-butadiene and formaldehyde, causing leukemia and lymphoma in adults and children.[27]

Fossil Fuel Extraction: Fracking

Fracking, the extraction of gas and oil from underground shale deposits by hydraulic fracturing, is a chemically intensive process, involving chemicals that are harmful to both reproduction and development.[28] Fracking operations release large quantities of particulates and toxic chemicals to air and water. These pollutants have potential to cause respiratory disease, cardiovascular disease, and cancer, as well as kidney, liver and neurological damage.[29] Epidemiological studies conducted among persons born or living near fracking sites have found health impacts in infants, including preterm birth and reduced birth weight,[30] elevated rates of childhood cancer, especially leukemia, and congenital heart defects.[31]

---

[27] Julia E. Heck, Andrew S. Park, Jiaheng Qiu, Myles Cockburn, and Beate Ritz, "Risk of Leukemia in Relation to Exposure to Ambient Air Toxics in Pregnancy and Early Childhood," *International Journal of Hygiene and Environmental Health* 217, no. 6 (2014): 662–668.

[28] Elise G. Elliott, Adrienne S. Ettinger, Brian P. Leaderer, Michael B. Bracken, and Nicole C. Deziel, "A Systematic Evaluation of Chemicals in Hydraulic-Fracturing Fluids and Wastewater for Reproductive and Developmental Toxicity," *Journal of Exposure Science & Environmental Epidemiology* 27, no. 1 (2017): 90–99.

[29] Lisa M. McKenzie, Roxana Z. Witter, Lee S. Newman, and John L. Adgate, "Human Health Risk Assessment of Air Emissions from Development of Unconventional Natural Gas Resources," *Science of the Total Environment* 424 (2012): 79–87.

[30] Elaine L. Hill and Lala Ma, "Drinking Water, Fracking, and Infant Health," *Journal of Health Economics* 82 (2022), doi.org/10.1016/j.jhealeco.2022.102595.

[31] Lisa M. McKenzie, William Allshouse, and Stephen Daniels, "Congenital Heart Defects and Intensity of Oil and Gas Well Site Activities in Early Pregnancy," *Environment International* 132 (2019), doi.org/10.1016/j.envint.2019.104949; Lisa M. McKenzie, William B. Allshouse, Tim E. Byers, Edward J. Bedrick, Berrin Serdar, and John L. Adgate, "Childhood Hematologic Cancer and Residential Proximity to Oil and Gas Development," *Plos One* 12, no. 2 (2017), doi.org/10.1371/journal.pone.0170423.

Petrochemical Refining, Ethane Cracking and Plastic Production

The large-scale industrial processes that convert fossil carbon into plastic expose workers and "fenceline" communities to multiple airborne pollutants and toxic chemicals including monomers (e.g., vinyl chloride, styrene and 1,3-butadiene), benzene, formaldehyde, toluene, phthalates and bisphenols. These materials are released into air, water and soil within workplaces and in neighboring communities.[32] Exposure to the carcinogens benzene and 1,3-butadiene causes leukemias and lymphomas.[33] Other chemical pollutants associated with plastic production increase risk of lung and breast cancer,[34] anemia, pre-term birth and low birth weight, asthma and other respiratory problems,[35] hypertension, heart disease, stroke, and kidney disease.[36]

Catastrophic Events

Plastic production is associated with extreme exposures that occur during catastrophic failures of the plastic production process, such as fires and

---

[32] Landrigan, et al., "The Minderoo-Monaco Commission on Plastics and Human Health."
[33] Heck, et al., "Risk of Leukemia in Relation to Exposure to Ambient Air Toxics in Pregnancy and Early Childhood."
[34] Cheng-Kuan Lin, Yu-Tien Hsu, David C. Christiani, Huei-Yang Hung, and Ro-Ting Lin, "Risks and Burden of Lung Cancer Incidence for Residential Petrochemical Industrial Complexes: A Meta-Analysis and Application," *Environment International* 121 (2018): 404–414.
[35] Montse Marquès, José L. Domingo, Martí Nadal, and Marta Schuhmacher, "Health Risks for the Population Living near Petrochemical Industrial Complexes. 2. Adverse Health Outcomes Other than Cancer," *Science of the Total Environment* 730 (2020), doi.org/10.1016/j.scitotenv.2020.139122.
[36] Ogochukwu Chinedum Okoye, Elaine Carnegie, and Luca Mora, "Air Pollution and Chronic Kidney Disease Risk in Oil and Gas- Situated Communities: A Systematic Review and Meta-Analysis," *International Journal of Public Health* 67 (2022): 1604522, doi.org/10.3389/ijph.2022.1604522.

explosions,[37] oil spills, and chemical spills. These events are associated with burns, traumatic injuries, and loss of life, as well as with massive releases of toxic materials to the environment.

Human Health Impacts of Plastic Recycling and Waste Disposal

An estimated 350 million tons of plastic waste are produced globally each year, and an estimated six billion tons, seventy-five percent of all plastic ever made, pollute the planet.[38] This waste causes extensive contamination of the environment, including the ocean,[39] and it threatens the lives of two billion people worldwide with eleven million waste pickers lacking safe workplaces and protective equipment.[40] Strategies for end-of-life waste management of plastic waste include both formal and informal recycling, landfilling, controlled and uncontrolled burning. All of these result in release of hazardous materials to the environment[41] and human exposure.

---

[37] Bluefield Process Safety, "External Plant Fires: What's the Likelihood?" (2017), www.bluefieldsafety.com/2017/09/external-plant-fires-whats-the-likelihood/; Pipeline and Hazardous Materials Safety Administration (PHMSA), and US Department of Transportation, "Pipeline Incident 20 Year Trends" (2022), www.phmsa.dot.gov/data-and-statistics/pipeline/pipeline-incident-20-year-trends.
[38] Roland Geyer, Jenna R. Jambeck, and Kara L. Law, "Production, Use, and Fate of All Plastics Ever Made," *Science Advances* 3, no. 7 (2017), doi.org/10.1126/sciadv.1700782.
[39] Richard C. Thompson, Ylva Olsen, Richard P. Mitchell, Anthony Davis, Steven J. Rowland, Anthony W. G. John, et al., "Lost at Sea: Where Is All the Plastic?" *Science* 304, no. 5672 (2004): 838–838.
[40] Costas A. Velis and Ed Cook, "Mismanagement of Plastic Waste Through Open Burning with Emphasis on the Global South: A Systematic Review of Risks to Occupational and Public Health," *Environmental Science & Technology* 55, no. 11 (2021): 7186–7207.
[41] Organisation for Economic Co-operation and Development (OECD), *Global Plastics Outlook: Economic Drivers, Environmental Impacts and Policy Options* (OECD Publishing, 2022).

Recycling

Plastic recycling, known variously as chemical recycling, mechanical recycling, enhanced recycling, pyrolysis, and upcycling is highly ineffective. Despite exaggerated claims by the plastic industry about the effectiveness of recycling, less than ten percent of all plastic is recycled globally. Plastic recycling and reuse lags far behind paper, glass, and aluminum recycling. Toxic chemical content and complexity are the major impediments.[42] Different polymers cannot be commingled in making recycled products, and recycled plastics cannot safely be incorporated into materials such as food packaging, clothing, or children's toys because they contain toxic chemicals.[43] For example, black plastic products made from recycled e-waste contain high concentrations of flame retardants including legacy flame retardants.[44]

Landfilling

Landfills containing waste plastic generate airborne gas emissions and cause contamination of ground and surface water by plastic-associated chemicals such as benzene, toluene, ethylbenzene, xylene and naphthalene.[45] Residential proximity to a landfill increases cancer risk.

---

[42] Landrigan, et al., "The Minderoo-Monaco Commission on Plastics and Human Health."

[43] Birgit Geueke, Drake W. Phelps, Lindsey V. Parkinson, and Jane Muncke, "Hazardous Chemicals in Recycled and Reusable Plastic Food Packaging," *Cambridge Prisms: Plastics* 1, no. e7 (2023), doi.org/10.1017/plc.2023.7.

[44] Megan Liu, Sicco H. Brandsma, and Erika Schreder, "From E-Waste to Living Space: Flame Retardants Contaminating Household Items Add to Concern About Plastic Recycling," *Chemosphere* 365 (2024): 143319, doi.org/10.1016/j.chemosphere.2024.143319.

[45] Ayesha Siddiqua, John N. Hahladakis, and Wadha Ahmed K. A. Al-Attiya, "An Overview of the Environmental Pollution and Health Effects Associated with Waste Landfilling and Open Dumping," *Environmental Science and Pollution Research* 29, no. 39 (2022): 58514–58536.

E-Waste

Electronic waste (e-waste), which consists largely of plastics plus thousands of other petrochemicals and metals, results in exposure to a wide range of hazardous materials including flame retardants, plasticizers, bisphenols, dioxins, toxic metals and particulate matter.[46] Additional toxic pollutants are produced when e-waste burns. E-waste's greatest hazards are seen at enormous e-waste disposal sites located in low-income and middle-income countries. Pregnant women and children are severely affected, and health effects include stillbirth, preterm birth, lower birth weight, reduced cognition, loss of IQ points, ADHD and behavioral problems.[47] Further impacts are decreased immune function and changed thyroid function as well as compromised lung function, respiratory symptoms, and asthma. Chronic diseases appearing later in life are also common and include cancer, cardiovascular disease, obesity, and osteoporosis.[48]

Incineration

Uncontrolled burning of plastic waste is a major source of pollution, especially in low- and middle-income countries. It generates airborne particulate matter and a wide range of hazardous chemicals including heavy metals, volatile organic compounds, toxic gases, and dioxins.[49] Health impacts include endocrine disruption, reproductive and

---

[46] Chunmiao M. Jia, Pallab Das, Insup Kim, Yong-Jin Yoon, Chor Yong Tay, and Jong-Min Lee, "Applications, Treatments, and Reuse of Plastics from Electrical and Electronic Equipment," *Journal of Industrial and Engineering Chemistry* 110 (2022): 84–99.

[47] World Health Organization, "Children and Digital Dumpsites" (2021), iris.who.int/handle/10665/341718.

[48] World Health Organization, "Children and Digital Dumpsites."

[49] Okunola A. Alabi, Kehinde I. Ologbonjaye, Oluwaseun Awosolu, and Olufiropo E. Alalade, "Public and Environmental Health Effects of Plastic Wastes Disposal: A Review," *Journal of Toxicology and Risk Assessment* 5, no. 1 (2019), doi.org/10.23937/2572-4061.1510021.

developmental disorders, altered thyroid function, increased risk of cognitive defects, respiratory and cutaneous symptoms, and cancer.[50]

Human Health Impacts from the Use of Plastics Products

Plastic Releases Harmful Chemicals

The more than 16,000 chemicals involved in plastics production include those added intentionally to impart functionality, such as plasticizers, flame retardants, UV light stabilizers, and heat stabilizers, as well as "non-intentionally added substances" (NIAS).[51] More than 4,200 plastic additives are chemicals of concern of which approximately 3,600 are not regulated globally. Moreover, no hazard information is available for over ten thousand plastic additives.[52] NIAS include impurities, contaminants from machinery, as well as degradation and transformation products of the original constituent chemicals. Impacts are also seen from plastic polymers themselves in terms of the constituent chemicals, human exposure and health impacts.[53]

Plastic additives, unreacted monomers, and NIAS are for the most part not chemically bonded to the polymer matrix and can leach out of plastic

---

[50] Landrigan, et al., "The Minderoo-Monaco Commission on Plastics and Human Health."
[51] United Nations Environment Programme (UNEP), and Secretariat of the Basel, Rotterdam, and Stockholm Conventions, "Chemicals in Plastics: A Technical Report" (2023), www.unep.org/resources/report/chemicals-plastics-technical-report; Helene Wiesinger, Zhanyun Y. Wang, and Stefanie Hellweg, "Deep Dive into Plastic Monomers, Additives, and Processing Aids," *Environmental Science & Technology* 55, no. 13 (2021): 9339–9351.
[52] Martin Wagner, Laura Monclús, Hans Peter H. Arp, et al., *State of the Science on Plastic Chemicals: Identifying and Addressing Chemicals and Polymers of Concern* (2024), zenodo.org/records/10701706.
[53] Bhedita J. Seewoo, Enoch V. S. Wong, Yannick R. Mulders, Louise M. Goodes, Ela Eroglu, Manuel Brunner, et al., "Impacts Associated with the Plastic Polymers Polycarbonate, Polystyrene, Polyvinyl Chloride, and Polybutadiene Across Their Life Cycle: A Review," *Heliyon* 10, no. 12 (2024), doi.org/10.1016/j.heliyon.2024.e32912.

products such as drink containers, food containers,[54] and baby food pouches.[55] They contaminate air, food, water, house dust, and the food chain, and they enter the bodies of living organisms, including humans.

Plastic Chemicals Are Ubiquitous in the Human Body

Plastic chemicals are found in seminal fluid,[56] follicular fluid, amniotic fluid, cord blood,[57] meconium,[58] children's and adult's blood and urine,[59] breast milk, and hair,[60] as well as in solid tissues such as liver, brain, breast

---

[54] Lisa Zimmermann, Martin Scheringer, Birgit Geueke, Justin M. Boucher, Lindsey V. Parkinson, Ksenia J. Groh, and Jane Muncke, "Implementing the EU Chemicals Strategy for Sustainability: The Case of Food Contact Chemicals of Concern," *Journal of Hazardous Materials* 437 (2022), doi.org/10.1016/j.jhazmat.2022.129167.

[55] Cheng Tang, Maria Jose Gomez Ramos, Amy Heffernan, Sarit Kaserzon, Cassandra Rauert, Chun-Yin Lin, et al., "Evaluation and Identification of Chemical Migrants Leached from Baby Food Pouch Packaging," *Chemosphere* 340 (2023): 139758, doi.org/10.1016/j.chemosphere.2023.139758.

[56] Elena Sánchez-Resino, Montse Marquès, Daniel Gutiérrez-Martín, Esteban Restrepo-Montes, Maria Angeles Martínez, Albert Salas-Huetos, et al., "Exploring the Occurrence of Organic Contaminants in Human Semen Through an Innovative Lc-Hrms-Based Methodology Suitable for Target and Nontarget Analysis," *Environmental Science & Technology* 57, no. 48 (2023): 19236–19252.

[57] Merve Buke Sahin, Murat Cagan, Anil Yirun, Aylin Balci Ozyurt, Selinay Basak Erdemli Kose, Irem Iyigun, et al., "Bisphenol Derivatives in Cord Blood and Association between Thyroid Hormones and Potential Exposure Sources," *International Journal of Environmental Health Research* 34, no. 8 (2024): 3036–3045.

[58] JiaLin Guo, Min Wu, Xi Gao, JingSi Chen, ShuGuang Li, Bo Chen, and RuiHua Dong, "Meconium Exposure to Phthalates, Sex and Thyroid Hormones, Birth Size, and Pregnancy Outcomes in 251 Mother-Infant Pairs from Shanghai," *International Journal of Environmental Research and Public Health* 17, no. 21 (2020), doi.org/10.3390/ijerph17217711.

[59] Christos Symeonides, Edoardo Aromataris, Yannick Mulders, Janine Dizon, Cindy Stern, Timothy Hugh Barker, et al., "An Umbrella Review of Meta-Analyses Evaluating Associations Between Human Health and Exposure to Major Classes of Plastic-Associated Chemicals," *Annals of Global Health* 90, no. 1 (2024), doi.org/10.5334/aogh.4459.

[60] Zhenwu Tang, Qifei Huang, Jiali Cheng, Yufei Yang, Jun Yang, Wei Guo, et al., "Polybrominated Diphenyl Ethers in Soils, Sediments, and Human Hair in a Plastic

tissue, and adipose tissue. National biomonitoring surveys detect several hundred plastic-associated chemicals in the bodies of virtually all humans of all ages.[61]

Impacts of Plastic Chemicals on Human Health

A large and growing body of evidence indicates that chemicals from plastic products are responsible for disease, disability, and premature death. These harms to health result in very large economic costs, and these impacts fall disproportionately on the poor and the vulnerable. Five classes of plastics chemicals—i.e., the monomer Bisphenol A (BPA), phthalate plasticisers, polychlorinated biphenyl (PCBs) flame retardants, and their polybrominated diphenyl ether (PBDEs) replacements—as well as some perfluoroalkyl and polyfluoroalkyl substances (PFAS) have been especially closely studied. Quantitative analysis encompassing ~1,000 meta-analyses of ~1.5m men, women and children exposed to one or more of these five chemicals and chemical classes shows consistent and statistically significant (95%) evidence for harm to human health.[62]

Health impacts of plastics chemicals in infants include miscarriage, and reduced birthweight, which diminishes children's ability to thrive and increases early mortality. In children, harms include IQ loss, asthma, obesity, insulin resistance (leading to type 2 diabetes) and high blood pressure (leading to cardiovascular disease). Harms in adults include type II diabetes, obesity, cardiovascular disease and cancer.[63] Recent hybrid epidemiological studies have reported that BPA exposure during

---

Waste Recycling Area: A Neglected Heavily Polluted Area," *Environmental Science & Technology* 48, no. 3 (2014): 1508–1516.
[61] US Centers for Disease Control and Prevention, "National Biomonitoring Program," (2024), www.cdc.gov/biomonitoring/index.html.
[62] Symeonides, et al., "An Umbrella Review of Meta-Analyses Evaluating Associations between Human Health and Exposure to Major Classes of Plastic-Associated Chemicals."
[63] Symeonides, et al., "An Umbrella Review of Meta-Analyses Evaluating Associations between Human Health and Exposure to Major Classes of Plastic-Associated Chemicals."

pregnancy acts through genetic and testosterone metabolic pathways to increase risk of autism in boys by over three-fold at age two and over six-fold at age nine.[64] Plastic-associated chemicals have negative impacts also on human reproduction, which include reduced sperm counts, sperm DNA damage, male and female reproductive birth defects, endometriosis, and polycystic ovarian syndrome.

The majority of chemicals in plastics have not been tested for toxicity, and therefore no information is available on their potential harms to human health.[65] Examination of approximately 1500 chemicals commonly used in plastic, comprising bisphenols, plasticisers, flame retardants, some PFAS and polymers, found that fewer than twenty-five percent have been studied in humans.[66] Equally concerning, chemicals identified as being harmful to human health are too often replaced by other chemicals that are also harmful, a process termed "regrettable substitution." Examples include replacement of BPA with its analogues Bisphenol S and Bisphenol F,[67] and replacement of flame-retardant PCBs with PBDEs[68] and organophosphorus flame retardants.[69]

---

[64] Christos Symeonides, Kristina Vacy, Sarah Thomson, Sam Tanner, Hui Kheng Chua, Shilpi Dixit, et al., "Male Autism Spectrum Disorder Is Linked to Brain Aromatase Disruption by Prenatal BPA in Multimodal Investigations and 10HDA Ameliorates the Related Mouse Phenotype," *Nature Communications* 15, no. 1 (2024), doi.org/10.1038/s41467-024-48897-8.

[65] Wagner, et al., *State of the Science on Plastic Chemicals: Identifying and Addressing Chemicals and Polymers of Concern.*

[66] Bhedita J. Seewoo, Louise M. Goodes, Louise Moffin, Yannick R. Mulders, Enoch V. S. Wong, Priyanka Toshniwal, et al., "The Plastic Health Map: A Systematic Evidence Map of Human Health Studies on Plastic-Associated Chemicals," *Environment International* 181 (2023), doi.org/10.1016/j.envint.2023.108225.

[67] Katherine Pelch, Jessica A. Wignall, Alexandra E. Goldstone, Pam K. Ross, Robyn B. Blain, Andrew J. Shapiro, et al., "A Scoping Review of the Health and Toxicological Activity of Bisphenol-a (BPA) Structural Analogues and Functional Alternatives," *Toxicology* 424 (2019), doi.org/10.1016/j.tox.2019.06.006.

[68] Symeonides, et al., "An Umbrella Review of Meta-Analyses Evaluating Associations between Human Health and Exposure to Major Classes of Plastic-Associated Chemicals."

[69] Zohra Chupeau, Nathalie Bonvallot, Fabien Mercier, Barbara Le Bot, Cecile Chevrier, and Philippe Glorennec, "Organophosphorus Flame Retardants: A Global Review of

Another concern is that most epidemiological studies evaluate the health impacts of only one plastic chemical (e.g., BPA) or one class of chemicals (e.g., phthalates) at a time. In reality, however, humans including pregnant women and newborn infants are exposed to mixtures of chemical which often act through similar biological pathways, such as endocrine disruption.[70] Little information is available as to whether these whether chemical mixture interactions are additive, antagonistic, or synergistic.

Plastics Break Down into Chemically Laden Micro- and Nanoplastic Particles

Plastics break down during use and following disposal into the environment into small particles (micro- and nanoplastics [MNPs]).[71] Sources of MNPs include everyday products such as water bottles, teabags, food packaging,[72] synthetic textiles and recycling,[73] as well as landfills and

---

Indoor Contamination and Human Exposure in Europe and Epidemiological Evidence," *International Journal of Environmental Research and Public Health* 17, no. 18 (2020), doi.org/10.3390/ijerph17186713.

[70] Nicolò Caporale, Michelle Leemans, Lina Birgersson, Pierre-Luc Germain, Cristina Cheroni, Gábor Borbély, et al., "From Cohorts to Molecules: Adverse Impacts of Endocrine Disrupting Mixtures," *Science* 375, no. 6582 (2022): 735, doi.org/10.1126/science.abe8244.

[71] Richard C. Thompson, Winnie Courtene-Jones, Julien Boucher, Sabine Pahl, Karen Raubenheimer, and Albert A. Koelmans, "Twenty Years of Microplastic Pollution Research: What Have We Learned?" *Science* 386, no. 6720 (2024), doi.org/10.1126/science.adl2746.

[72] Yang Yu, Nicholas Craig, and Lei Su, "A Hidden Pathway for Human Exposure to Micro- and Nanoplastics—The Mechanical Fragmentation of Plastic Products During Daily Use," *Toxics* 11, no. 9 (2023), doi.org/10.3390/toxics11090774.

[73] Michael J. Stapleton, Ashley J. Ansari, Aziz Ahmed, and Faisal I. Hai, "Evaluating the Generation of Microplastics from an Unlikely Source: The Unintentional Consequence of the Current Plastic Recycling Process," *Science of the Total Environment* 902 (2023), doi.org/10.1016/j.scitotenv.2023.166090; Go Suzuki, Natsuyo Uchida, Kosuke Tanaka, Osamu Higashi, Yusuke Takahashi, Hidetoshi Kuramochi, et al., "Global Discharge of

informal dumpsites.[74] MNPs are disseminated globally in the air, the ocean, fresh water, soil, household dust, food and drink, and they act as sources of human exposure.[75] MNPs leach their constituent chemicals—i.e., plastic additives and NIAS—into the environment and into living organisms, including humans.[76] They act also as vectors of contaminants including heavy metals and pesticides as well as of pathogenic bacteria.[77]

Chemical-laden MNPs Enter the Human Body and May Harm Health

MNPs are increasingly detected in human tissue. Reflecting inhalation and ingestion as major exposure routes, microplastics have been reported

---

Microplastics from Mechanical Recycling of Plastic Waste," *Environmental Pollution* 348 (2024), doi.org/10.1016/j.envpol.2024.123855.

[74] Mosarrat Samiha Kabir, Hong Wang, Stephanie Luster-Teasley, Lifeng Zhang, and Renzun Zhao, "Microplastics in Landfill Leachate: Sources, Detection, Occurrence, and Removal," *Environmental Science and Ecotechnology* 16 (2023), doi.org/10.1016/j.ese.2023.100256; Seewoo, et al., "Impacts Associated with the Plastic Polymers Polycarbonate, Polystyrene, Polyvinyl Chloride, and Polybutadiene across Their Life Cycle: A Review"; Yong Wan, Xin Chen, Qian Liu, Hongjuan Hu, Chenxi Wu, and Qiang Xue, "Informal Landfill Contributes to the Pollution of Microplastics in the Surrounding Environment," *Environmental Pollution* 293 (2022), doi.org/10.1016/j.envpol.2021.118586.

[75] World Health Organization, "Microplastics in Drinking-Water" (2019), www.who.int/publications/i/item/9789241516198; World Health Organization, "Dietary and Inhalation Exposure to Nano- and Microplastic Particles and Potential Implications for Human Health" (2022), www.who.int/publications/i/item/9789240054608.

[76] Yage Li, Chen Liu, Haotian Yang, Wenhui He, Beibei Li, Xinyi Zhu, et al., "Leaching of Chemicals from Microplastics: A Review of Chemical Types, Leaching Mechanisms, and Influencing Factors," *Science of the Total Environment* 906 (2024), doi.org/10.1016/j.scitotenv.2023.167666.

[77] Vasiliki Kinigopoulou, Ioannis Pashalidis, Dimitrios Kalderis, and Ioannis Anastopoulos, "Microplastics as Carriers of Inorganic and Organic Contaminants in the Environment: A Review of Recent Progress," *Journal of Molecular Liquids* 350 (2022), doi.org/10.1016/j.molliq.2022.118580.

in lung and gut,[78] but also in placenta, breast milk, blood, testes and brain.[79] These reports require verification as measurement techniques continue to be refined.

Evidence of human health impacts from MNPs is beginning to emerge. Synthetic textile workers occupationally exposed to high levels of microplastics suffer a wide range of lung diseases, including shortness of breath, cough, respiratory failure, as well as lung and large bowel cancer.[80] Fecal microplastic load is reported to correlate with the severity of inflammatory bowel disease[81] and liver cirrhosis.[82] Patients with MNPs in carotid arterial plaques had a four-fold increased risk of myocardial infarction, stroke, or death from any cause compared to those in whom MNPs were not detected.[83] While measurement techniques have limitations, an increasing body of *in vitro* and animal laboratory studies link MNPs to a wide range of harmful impacts including inflammation

---

[78] Luis Fernando Amato-Lourenço, Regiani Carvalho-Oliveira, Gabriel Ribeiro, Luciana dos Santos Galvao, Romulo Augusto Ando, and Thais Mauad, "Presence of Airborne Microplastics in Human Lung Tissue," *Journal of Hazardous Materials* 416 (2021), doi.org/10.1016/j.jhazmat.2021.126124.

[79] Marthinus Brits, Martin J. M. van Velzen, Feride Öykü Sefiloglu, Lorenzo Scibetta, Quinn Groenewoud, Juan J. Garcia-Vallejo, et al., "Quantitation of Micro and Nanoplastics in Human Blood by Pyrolysis-Gas Chromatography-Mass Spectrometry," *Microplastics and Nanoplastics* 4, no. 1 (2024): 12, doi.org/10.1186/s43591-024-00090-w; Thompson, et al., "Twenty Years of Microplastic Pollution Research: What Have We Learned?"

[80] Joana C. Prata, "Airborne Microplastics: Consequences to Human Health?" *Environmental Pollution* 234 (2018): 115–126.

[81] Zehua H. Yan, Yafei F. Liu, Ting Zhang, Faming M. Zhang, Hongqiang Ren, and Yan Zhang, "Analysis of Microplastics in Human Feces Reveals a Correlation between Fecal Microplastics and Inflammatory Bowel Disease Status," *Environmental Science & Technology* 56, no. 1 (2022): 414–421.

[82] Thomas Horvatits, Matthias Tamminga, Beibei Liu, Marcial Sebode, Antonella Carambia, Lutz Fischer, et al., "Microplastics Detected in Cirrhotic Liver Tissue," *Ebiomedicine* 82 (2022), doi.org/10.1016/j.ebiom.2022.104147.

[83] Raffaele Marfella, Francesco Prattichizzo, Celestino Sardu, Gianluca Fulgenzi, Laura Graciotti, Tatiana Spadoni, et al., "Microplastics and Nanoplastics in Atheromas and Cardiovascular Events," *New England Journal of Medicine* 390, no. 10 (2024): 900–910.

and oxidative stress.[84] In light of this growing evidence, a precautionary regulatory approach is absolutely critical.[85]

Plastic and Social Justice

Plastics' harms to health are not evenly or fairly distributed. In addition to disproportionately harming children, plastics' harms are inequitably distributed amongst adults. Groups especially heavily exposed include people of color, Indigenous populations, fossil fuel extraction workers, chemical and plastic production workers, informal waste and recovery workers, and persons living in "fenceline" communities adjacent to fossil fuel extraction, plastic production, and plastic waste facilities. These groups experience disproportionately high risks of disease, disability, and death caused by plastic as well as experience increased risks of premature birth, low birth weight, asthma, leukemia, cardiovascular disease, chronic obstructive pulmonary disease, and lung cancer.

Economic Impacts of Plastic Production

The disease and premature death caused by plastics result in major economic costs. These health-related losses fall into two categories: health care costs and productivity costs resulting from lost income due to disease, disability, and premature death. The Minderoo-Monaco Commission analysed these health-related costs for the year 2015 and estimated that the health-related costs of plastic production were $592 billion (in PPP dollars) globally.[86] The Commission found additionally that the costs of disease linked to

---

[84] Arifur Rahman, Atanu Sarkar, Om Prakash Yadav, Gopal Achari, and Jaroslav Slobodnik, "Potential Human Health Risks Due to Environmental Exposure to Nano-and Microplastics and Knowledge Gaps: A Scoping Review," *Science of the Total Environment* 757 (2021), doi.org/10.1016/j.scitotenv.2020.143872.
[85] Thompson, et al., "Twenty Years of Microplastic Pollution Research: What Have We Learned?"
[86] Landrigan, et al., "The Minderoo-Monaco Commission on Plastics and Human Health."

three plastic chemicals were $675 billion in the USA alone: diethyl hexyl ortho-phthalate (DEHP) plasticiser for all-cause mortality, PBDEs flame retardants for IQ point loss in children, and BPA for heart-attack and stroke.[87] The total annual health-related economic losses related to plastic in 2015 were thus $1.2 trillion.[88]

A more recent study examining the health-related costs associated with the same three plastic-associated chemicals but for a much larger population—i.e., thirty-eight countries amounting to one third of the world's population—put these estimates even higher at around $1.5 trillion.[89] Another study on the same chemical classes estimated that disease and associated costs were equivalent to 1.22% of the US gross domestic product.[90] Estimated health costs of PFAS exposure in the US were approximately $22 billion in 2018.[91]

The Minderoo-Monaco Commission noted that these economic estimates substantially undercount the full costs of disease and death caused by plastics, since they are based on only a subset of the exposed global population, cover only a fraction of the chemicals known to be used in plastic, and are limited to those health outcomes that to date have been recognized and quantified. Moreover, they consider the consequences of exposures to only one chemical at a time, while in reality humans are simultaneously exposed to multiple chemicals[92] and the possibly

---

[87] Landrigan, et al., "The Minderoo-Monaco Commission on Plastics and Human Health."
[88] Landrigan, et al., "The Minderoo-Monaco Commission on Plastics and Human Health."
[89] Maureen Cropper, Sarah Dunlop, Hudson Hinshaw, Philip Landrigan, Yongjoon Park, and Christos Symeonides, "The Benefits of Removing Toxic Chemicals from Plastics," *Proceedings of the National Academy of Sciences of the United States of America* 121, no. 52 (2024), doi.org/10.1073/pnas.2412714121.
[90] Leonardo Trasande, Roopa Krithivasan, Kevin Park, Vladislav Obsekov, and Michael Belliveau, "Chemicals Used in Plastic Materials: An Estimate of the Attributable Disease Burden and Costs in the United States," *Journal of the Endocrine Society* 8, no. 2 (2024), doi.org/10.1210/jendso/bvad163.
[91] Trasande, et al., "Chemicals Used in Plastic Materials."
[92] Aolin L. Wang, Dimitri Panagopoulos Abrahamsson, Ting Jiang, Miaomiao Wang, Rachel Morello-Frosch, June-Soo Park, et al., "Suspect Screening, Prioritization, and

synergistic health effects of these multiple, simultaneous exposures have not yet been examined.

Hence, the health-related costs of plastics are largely externalized by the plastic production industry and imposed on governments, taxpayers, and individual citizens.

Polymer Production is Heavily Subsidised

Governments in many countries provide major subsidies and tax breaks for fossil fuel feedstock extraction, energy generation, and polymerisation. Global estimates of the magnitude of these subsidies are $43 billion in 2024 rising to $78 billion by 2050.[93] Saudi Arabia accounted for the majority at $38 billion in 2024 and $64 billion in 2050. Modelling suggests that removing subsidies for plastic production would increase consumer prices only minimally (bottled water: 0.75%; bottled soft drink: 0.17%; clothing: 0.16%; flooring 1.53%; agriculture 3.16%).[94]

The human health costs resulting from exposures to plastic-associated chemicals are much larger than the subsidies provided by governments to plastic producers. This creates an ethical imbalance in which plastic producers and fossil fuel corporations are rewarded economically for creating harms to health that fall disproportionately on the poorest and most vulnerable members of societies.

Confirmation of Environmental Chemicals in Maternal-Newborn Pairs from San Francisco," *Environmental Science & Technology* 55, no. 8 (2021): 5037–5049.

[93] Eunomia and Quaker United Nations Office (QUNO), "Plastic Money: Turning Off the Subsidies Tap. Phase 2 Report," (2024), eunomia.eco/wp-content/uploads/2024/11/Plastic-Production-Subsidies-Modelling-Phase-2-report-v1.0.pdf.

[94] Eunomia and Quaker United Nations Office (QUNO), "Plastic Money."

Plastic Production Is Increasing Exponentially

Relentless increases in production are the main driver of plastics' worsening harms to human health and the global environment. Global plastic output has grown over 200-fold; from two million tons in 1950 to more than 450 million tons today. It is projected to double again by 2040 and treble by 2060 (Figure 1). Single-use plastic accounts for thirty-five to forty percent of current production, is the most rapidly growing fraction of plastic manufacture, and contributes disproportionately to plastic waste.[95] As plastic production continues to grow, so does plastic pollution with a strong log-log linear relationship between the two.[96]

---

[95] Organisation for Economic Co-operation and Development (OECD), *Global Plastics Outlook: Economic Drivers, Environmental Impacts and Policy Options*; Organisation for Economic Co-operation and Development (OECD), *Global Plastics Outlook: Policy Scenarios to 2060* (OECD Publishing, 2022).

[96] Win Cowger, Kathryn A. Willis, Sybil Bullock, Katie Conlon, Jorge Emmanuel, Lis M. Erdle, et al., "Global Producer Responsibility for Plastic Pollution," *Science Advances* 10, no. 17 (2024), doi.org/10.1126/sciadv.adj8275; Paul Stegmann, Vassilis Daioglou, Marc Londo, Detlef P. P. van Vuuren, and Martin Junginger, "Plastic Futures and Their Co-Emissions," *Nature* 612, no. 7939 (2022): 272–276.

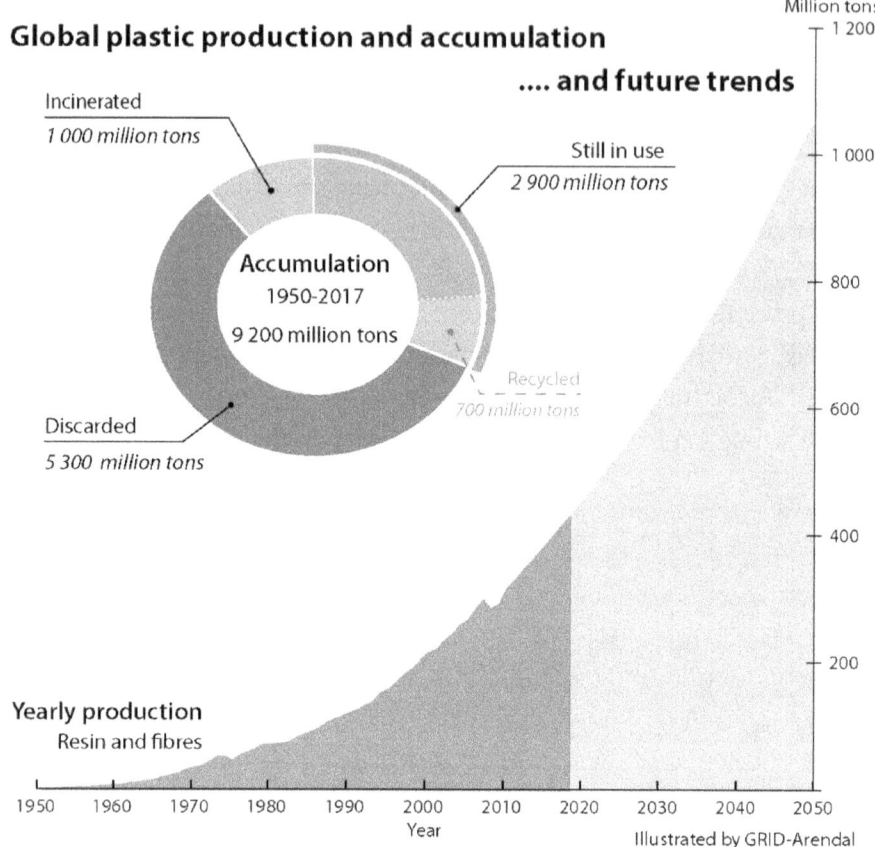

UNEP (2021). From Pollution to Solution: A global assessment of marine litter and plastic pollution. Nairobi.

Figure 1.

Solutions

Technical Solutions

To address the global plastics crisis and reduce plastics' harms to human health and the environment, nations and states have begun to pass laws and implement policies.

Safeguarding Human Health Against Plastics and Petrochemicals

Since 2008, Rwanda has banned the manufacture, import, and use of plastic bags.[97] In February 2020, Rwanda launched an awareness campaign for ending single use plastics such as disposable dishes, plastic bottles, straws, coffee stirrers, and disposable cutlery. This was followed by a legal ban on single-use plastics in 2019. These laws are supported by strict enforcement and severe penalties. They have resulted in nationwide reduction in plastic pollution.

California legislation enacted in 2022 (SB 54) will require plastic producers to pay $500 million a year for ten years starting in 2027 for environmental mitigation and to address harms caused by plastics to disadvantaged, low-income, and rural communities.[98] California also passed legislation (SB 1137) to protect the health of California's "fenceline" communities by creating a minimum health and safety distance of 3,200 feet between sensitive receptors (such as a residences, schools, childcare facilities, playgrounds, hospitals, and nursing homes) and oil and gas production wells.[99]

To bring these actions to global scale, the UN Environment Assembly adopted a historic resolution on March 2, 2022, to develop a global plastics treaty. The stated goal of this treaty is to reduce plastic pollution, including ocean pollution and microplastics, across the entire plastic life cycle. Treaty negotiations are on a fast track. To date, an Intergovernmental Negotiating Committee (INC) has met five times with a sixth meeting scheduled for 2025. A plastics treaty that prioritizes protection of human health will contain two key provisions—a cap on production of new plastics and strict regulation of plastic-associated chemicals. More than one

---

[97] Janvier Hakuzimana, "Break Free from Plastics: Environmental Perspectives and Evidence from Rwanda," *Environment & Ecosystem Science* 5, no. 1 (2021): 27–36.

[98] California Legislative Information, "Senate Bill No. 54 Solid Waste: Reporting, Packaging, and Plastic Food Service Ware" (2022), leginfo.legislature.ca.gov/faces/billTextClient.xhtml?bill_id=202120220SB54.

[99] California Legislative Information, "Senate Bill No. 1137 Oil and Gas: Operations: Location Restrictions: Notice of Intention: Health Protection Zone: Sensitive Receptors" (2022), leginfo.legislature.ca.gov/faces/billTextClient.xhtml?bill_id=202120220SB1137.

hundred nations, the High Ambition Coalition, support these provisions in the treaty negotiations. However, the plastics and petrochemical industries as well as major petrostates, led by Saudi Arabia and Russia, oppose these provisions. Negotiations will continue in 2025.

Sustainable Solutions

Technical and legal solutions to planetary problems such as the Global Plastics Treaty are important, necessary, and frequently effective, as seen in the sharp declines in chlorofluorocarbon manufacture that resulted from the Montreal Protocol,[100] reductions in air pollution following passage of national clean air laws,[101] and global bans on the manufacture of persistent organic pollutants under the Stockholm Convention.[102] All of these solutions have, however, been reactive. They have been developed only after recognition of a threat. None has looked beyond the problem at hand. None offers protection against hazards yet to come.

Sustainable protection against current and future dangers will require solutions that extend beyond specific threats. Such solutions go beyond one-off technical and legal solutions and address the underlying political, economic, and ethical causes of plastic pollution, climate change, and other components of the current planetary crisis. Likewise, assessment of the impacts of these deeper solutions will require metrics that go beyond

---

[100] Ashley Woodcock, "Hydrofluorocarbons, Climate, and Health: Moving the Montreal Protocol Beyond Ozone-Layer Recovery," *New England Journal of Medicine* 388, no. 26 (2023): 2404–2406.

[101] Jason Price, Sahil Gulati, Jacob Lehr, and Stefani Penn, "The Benefits and Costs of U.S. Air Pollution Regulations" (2020), https://www.nrdc.org/sites/default/files/iec-benefits-costs-us-air-pollution-regulations-report.pdf.

[102] Heidelore Fiedler, Roland Kallenborn, Jacob de Boer, and Leiv K. Sydnes, "The Stockholm Convention: A Tool for the Global Regulation of Persistent Organic Pollutants," *Chemistry International* 41, no. 2 (2019): 4–11.

gross domestic product (GDP) and explicitly value human and natural capital.[103]

In his 2015 encyclical letter *Laudato Si': On Care for Our Common Home,* the late Pope Francis (1936–2025) examines the current planetary crises, offers insights into their root causes, and suggests strategies for planetary restoration and regeneration. With the integration of science and theology, Francis breaks through the stereotype, dating to the time of Galileo Galilei (1564–1642), that there is an inherent conflict between science and religion, and he opens the way for new solutions based on both faith and reason. Drawing on science, Francis argues that there is "an urgent need" to reduce greenhouse gas emissions, control pollution, replace fossil fuels, and encourage the development of renewable energy.[104] Drawing on theology, he argues that climate change, pollution, and biodiversity loss are not only environmental problems, but also moral injustices—affronts to human dignity.

For Pope Francis, sustainable strategies for healing the planet must be based on both the best science and the most rigorous ethical analysis. These strategies need to be scientifically sound, and they need to be just. He urges humankind to move beyond one-off solutions, to examine the structures and metrics used to manage our economy, and to reimagine how these structures could be redesigned for the benefit of all. He states that every solution to the planetary crisis must incorporate "a preferential option for the poorest"[105] and restore "dignity to the excluded."[106] He terms this approach integral ecology. Integral ecology is a powerfully holistic concept that moves ecologic thinking beyond purely green concerns and puts people in the landscape. It is anchored in Francis' view that the Earth is a

---

[103] Pushpam Kumar, ed., *Mainstreaming Natural Capital and Ecosystem Services into Development Policy* (Routledge/Taylor & Francis Group, 2019).
[104] Francis, *Laudato Si'*, no. 26.
[105] Francis, *Laudato Si'*, no. 158.
[106] Francis, *Laudato Si'*, no. 139.

shared inheritance, a "common home," whose "fruits are meant to benefit everyone."[107]

Declaration

Acting on the recognition that the plastic crisis has an ethical and a moral dimension, the October 2024 Boston College conference, "Joining Science and Theology to End Plastic Pollution, Protect Health, and Advance Social Justice," issued a Declaration stating that:

> Continuing unchecked increases in plastic production are unethical and immoral.[4] They threaten all life on earth. Those who advocate for unchecked growth in plastics must re-examine their behavior, embrace the reality that the earth is a shared inheritance—a gift from the Creator, and work toward a more equitable and sustainable future. All of us have a shared responsibility to be good stewards of God's creation.[108]

This Declaration was endorsed by Prince Albert II of Monaco and by multiple religious leaders of many faiths, including the Dalai Lama, Patriarch Bartholomew of Constantinople, prominent rabbis, and Christian theologians—Catholic, mainstream Protestant, and evangelical Protestant—as well as women and men of faith who recognize humanity's responsibility to protect our small blue planet and protect all life.

Going forward, it is our hope that negotiations for the UN Global Plastics Treaty will incorporate the best science, consider the moral and ethical dimension of the plastic crisis, and act responsibly in light of those considerations to prioritize the protection of human health.

---

[107] Francis, *Laudato Si'*, no. 93.
[108] The Declaration can be found in Chapter 15 of this volume.

Sarah Dunlop, PhD, is Emerita Professor, University of Western Australia. Her medical research career focused on brain development and recovery following chemical and physical injury to the brain, spinal cord and peripheral nervous system, including randomised controlled trials. She joined Minderoo Foundation in 2020 to establish and lead the Plastics and Human Health Impact Mission. Dr. Dunlop's previous roles include Accorded Status, Royal Perth Hospital; Director, Spinal Cord Injury Network; President, Australian Neuroscience Society; President, Federation of Australasian & Oceanian Neuroscience Societies.

Yannick Mulders received his PhD from the University of Western Australia on research focusing on temperate reef ecology. He joined the Minderoo Foundation in 2021 and is Advisor Researcher in the Plastic and Human Health Impact Mission. He has co-authored multiple major publications such as the Plastic Health Map, the "Minderoo-Monaco Commission on Plastic and Human Health," and the "Plastic and Human Health Umbrella Review." He continues to work on innovative ways of accelerating the synthesis and dissemination of evidence of harm to human health across the entire lifecycle of plastic. His passion for investigating the effects of plastics on human health largely stems from his youth, when he lived in the fenceline community of a large petrochemical refinery.

Louise Goodes is a physiotherapist with extensive clinical research experience. She joined Minderoo in 2020 and is Principal Researcher in the Plastic and Human Health Impact Mission. She coordinates major scientific literature reviews such as the Plastic Health Map examining plastic chemical exposure and human health outcomes. Previous roles include Research Manager of the Western Australian Neurotrauma Research Program and Research Coordinator for the Western Australian arm of three multinational randomised controlled trials on Spinal Cord Injury and Physical Activity; she was also a clinical trial coordinator investigating biological therapies for bladder health in acute spinal cord injury.

Hervé Raps, MD, is the Research Delegate Physician at the Monaco Scientific Center, where he leads the Clinical Research support activity and the "Ocean and Human Health" theme. He is conducting awareness-raising and capacity-building activities on environmental health issues, particularly those related to the oceans, for a range of stakeholders. He has been on the steering committee and among the authors of the Monaco Commission on Ocean Pollution and Human Health and the Minderoo-Monaco Commission on Plastics and Human Health. He is a member of the Steering Committee of the "Espace Éthique PACA Corse" and the Scientific Council of Académie 3 at the Université Côte d'Azur in France.

Philip J. Landrigan, MD, MSc, FAAP, is Director of the Global Public Health and the Common Good program, and Director of the Global Observatory on Planetary Health at Boston College. Internationally, he collaborates with the Centre Scientifique de Monaco. He is a pediatrician, public health physician, and epidemiologist. Author of over seven hundred scientific publications and ten books, in his research he uses the tools of epidemiology to elucidate connections between toxic chemicals and human health, especially the health of infants and children. He is particularly interested in understanding how toxic chemicals injure the developing brains and nervous systems of children and in translating this knowledge into public policy to protect health. In New York City, he worked for many years in the Icahn School of Medicine at Mount Sinai and he was involved in the medical and epidemiologic follow-up of twenty thousand 9/11 rescue workers. From 2015 to 2017, he co-chaired the *Lancet* Commission on Pollution and Health. He is also member of the National Institute of Medicine.

Part 2

Assessing *the* Challenges

3. The Disproportionate Impacts of Plastics on Low- and Middle-Income Countries

Adetoun Mustapha Olaitan

Plastic pollution is a global problem, but its impacts are not felt equally. According to the OECD First Global Plastics Outlook, globally, only nine percent of plastic waste is recycled. Fifteen percent is collected for recycling but forty percent of that is disposed of as residues. Another nineteen percent is incinerated, fifty percent ends up in landfill, and twenty-two percent evades waste management systems and goes into uncontrolled dumpsites, is burned in open pits, or ends up in terrestrial or aquatic environments, especially in poorer countries.[1]

Issue of unmanaged and mismanaged plastic waste is especially acute in developing countries, where the infrastructure for collection, reuse, and recycling is often insufficient or lacking.[2] Plastic crisis is now exacerbated by growing imports of plastic waste from the high-income countries (HICs). Low- and Middle-Income Countries (LMICs) bear the brunt of plastic pollution's social, environmental, and economic consequences.[3]

Global North-South Divide

Plastic waste emissions are highest across countries in Southern Asia, Sub-Saharan Africa and Southeastern Asia. About sixty-nine percent (or 35.7

---

[1] See Organisation for Economic Co-operation and Development (OECD), *Global Plastics Outlook: Economic Drivers, Environmental Impacts and Policy Options* (OECD Publishing, 2022).
[2] See Shelby Browning, Betsy Beymer-Farris, and Jeffrey R. Seay, "Addressing the Challenges Associated with Plastic Waste Disposal and Management in Developing Countries," *Current Opinion in Chemical Engineering* 32 (2021), doi.org/10.1016/j.coche.2021.100682.
[3] See World Wide Fund for Nature (WWF), *Who Pays for Plastic Pollution? Enabling Global Equity in the Plastic Value Chain* (World Wide Fund for Nature, 2023).

million tonnes (Mt) per year) of the world's plastic pollution comes from twenty nations, none of which are high income countries. India burns roughly 5.8 Mt of plastic each year and releases another 3.5 Mt of plastics into the environment (land, air, water) as debris. Cumulatively, India contributes to 9.3 Mt of plastic pollution in the world annually, Nigeria (3.5 Mt), Indonesia (3.4 Mt), and China (2.8 Mt).[4] Despite the Global North having higher plastic waste generation rates than countries in the South, not a single high income country is "ranked in the top ninety polluters, because most have 100% collection coverage and controlled disposal."[5]

Social, Environmental, and Economic Consequences

Plastic pollution creates negative social, environmental and economic impact. It hurts livelihoods dependent on natural resources causing unemployment. It is estimated that eighty percent of plastics, including single-use products like earbuds, sweet wrappers, straws and coffee cup lids, have little or no value at the end of life. Pollution from this sector alone could greatly impact fisheries that employ over twelve million Africans.[6]

Plastic pollution desecrates cultural and historical sites and violates the right to a healthy environment. Waterways, soil, and air are already polluted with plastic wastes, harming ecosystems and wildlife. Plastic pollution of water bodies is a threat to the establishment of a vibrant blue economy.[7] Inadequate waste collection and disposal infrastructure lead to

---

[4] See Joshua W. Cottom, Ed Cook, and Costas A. Velis, "A Local-to-Global Emissions Inventory of Macroplastic Pollution," *Nature* 633, no. 8028 (2024): 101–108.
[5] Cottom, et al., "A Local-to-Global Emissions Inventory of Macroplastic Pollution," 103.
[6] See Swati Singh Sambyal, "Five African Countries among Top 20 Highest Contributors to Plastic Marine Debris in the World," *DownToEarth*, May 22, 2018, www.downtoearth.org.in/news/waste/when-oceans-fill-apart-60629.
[7] See Sambyal, "Five African Countries Among Top 20 Highest Contributors to Plastic Marine Debris in the World;" Jenna R. Jambeck, Britta Denise Hardesty, Amy L. Brooks, Tessa Friend, Kristian Teleki, Joan Fabres, et al., "Challenges and Emerging Solutions to the Land-Based Plastic Waste Issue in Africa," *Marine Policy* 96 (2018): 256–263.

plastic litter and open burning. Therefore, plastic production and its open burning contribute to greenhouse gas emissions, exacerbating climate change impacts.

The health impacts of plastics have been of concern. Plastic waste contaminates water sources and promotes the spread of diseases like malaria and cholera and an increased disease burden (e.g., respiratory issues, cancer, etc.).[8] It has been estimated that the impacts of plastic pollution cost up to one million lives each year in low- and middle-income countries.[9]

Social and Environmental Justice

Social and environmental justice focuses on the equitable distribution of both environmental resources and burdens so that no one group of people bears a disproportionate share of the negative consequences resulting from industrial operations and/or government policies.

The adverse effects of plastic pollution and climate change are widespread but currently felt most keenly in certain geographies and among certain groups and populations least responsible for the pollution who lack the power or resources needed to address these problems.[10] As a result, plastic pollution has been described as a new form of "colonialism."[11] Plastic pollution creates dire inequities for people, the environment, and countries, and prevents individuals and societies from flourishing. Environmental injustices occur at local, national, and global scales, including injustices occurring between the regions of the Global

---

[8] See World Wide Fund for Nature, *Who Pays for Plastic Pollution?*
[9] See Sambyal, "Five African Countries Among Top 20 Highest Contributors to Plastic Marine Debris in the World."
[10] See Katharine A. Owens and Katie Conlon, "Mopping Up or Turning Off the Tap? Environmental Injustice and the Ethics of Plastic Pollution," *Frontiers in Marine Science* 8 (2021), doi.org/10.3389/fmars.2021.713385.
[11] See Sedat Gündoğdu, ed., *Plastic Waste Trade: A New Colonialist Means of Pollution Transfer* (Springer, 2024).

North and Global South. Global North nations continue dumping waste in both domestic and global 'pollution havens' where the cost of doing business is much cheaper, regulation is virtually non-existent, and residents do not hold much formal political power.[12]

Gender Injustice and Impacts on Women Waste Pickers

Of the estimated twenty million waste pickers worldwide, the majority are women from socially and ethnically marginalized communities.[13] Unjustly, women waste pickers are often "invisible" or disrespected in their societies; they work long hours in unhealthy conditions and earn lower wages compared to men.[14] Limited attention is paid to the occupational health issues and social harms experienced by women waste pickers. Few studies from around the world report significant impacts on women as a result of consistent exposure to toxic plastic and electronic waste (e-waste), many of which contain known endocrine disruptors.[15]

---

[12] See Gündoğdu, *Plastic Waste Trade*; Randika Jayasinghe, "Waste Management in the Global North," in *The Garbage Crisis: A Global Challenge for Engineers*, ed. R. Jayasinghe, U. Mushtaq, T. A. Smythe, and C. Baillie, Synthesis Lectures on Engineers, Technology, & Society (Springer, 2013), 69–86.

[13] See Cecilia Allen, "An Inclusive Recovery: The Social, Environmental, & Economic Benefits of Partnering with Informal Recyclers," *Global Alliance for Incinerator Alternatives* (GAIA) (2021), www.no-burn.org/resources/an-inclusive-recovery-the-social-environmental-economic-benefits-of-partnering-with-informal-recyclers/; Global Alliance of Waste Pickers, "The International Alliance of Waste Pickers Position on Extended Producer Responsibility (EPR)" (2021), epr.globalrec.org/position-on-epr/#:~:text=EPR%20should%20maintain%20or%20establish,formal%20and%20decent%20labor%20conditions.

[14] See Philip J. Landrigan, Hervé Raps, Maureen Cropper, Caroline Bald, Manuel Brunner, Elvia Maya Canonizado, et al., "The Minderoo-Monaco Commission on Plastics and Human Health," *Annals of Global Health* 89, no. 1 (2023), doi.org/10.5334/aogh.4056.

[15] See Landrigan, et al., "The Minderoo-Monaco Commission on Plastics and Human Health;" Samuel Abalansa, Badr El Mahrad, John Icely, and Alice Newton, "Electronic Waste, an Environmental Problem Exported to Developing Countries: The Good, the Bad, and the Ugly," *Sustainability* 13, no. 9 (2021), doi.org/10.3390/su13095302; Saqib

Some Drivers of Plastic Pollution in LMICs

Population growth will drive a range of urbanization challenges across Africa's biggest cities, the most pressing of which include availability of clean, safe drinking water and the need to manage the waste footprint amid a limited recycling infrastructure. Due to lack of clean drinking water, single-use sachets are popularly used.[16] For example, in Nigeria, where only about twenty-nine percent of the population uses safely managed clean drinking water,[17] absence of potable drinking water has led to water sachets, heat-sealed plastic sleeves of drinking water, becoming the source of drinking water for millions of Nigerians. Its widespread consumption has led to plastic pollution due to inadequate waste management infrastructure and poor waste disposal behavior. There is an informal waste collection economy, but this favours rigid plastic and disregards low-weight plastic water sachets because waste pickers are paid by weight. The improper management of plastics coupled with infrastructure not growing at the same pace means that only half of plastic waste is currently collected and around ten percent is recycled.[18]

Plastic pollution is further exacerbated by the growing middle class in Africa, creating large markets for consumer plastic goods and packaging.[19]

Hassan, Aswin Thacharodi, Anshu Priya, R. Meenatchi, Thanushree A. Hegde, R. Thangamani, et al., "Endocrine Disruptors: Unravelling the Link between Chemical Exposure and Women's Reproductive Health," *Environmental Research* 241 (2024), doi.org/10.1016/j.envres.2023.117385.

[16] See United Nations Environmental Programme (UNEP), "The Rarely Told Story of the Widely Used Water Sachets," May 24, 2023, www.unep.org/news-and-stories/story/rarely-told-story-widely-used-water-sachets.

[17] See UN Water, "Nigeria: SDG 6 Snapshot in Nigeria," www.sdg6data.org/en/country-or-area/nigeria.

[18] See Sunil Kumar, Stephen R. Smith, Geoff Fowler, Costas Velis, S. Jyoti Kumar, Shashi Arya, et al., "Challenges and Opportunities Associated with Waste Management in India," *Royal Society Open Science* 4, no. 3 (2017), doi.org/10.1098/rsos.160764.

[19] See Sambyal, "Five African Countries Among Top 20 Highest Contributors to Plastic Marine Debris in the World."

Waste mismanagement is associated with a lack of infrastructure in many African countries.[20]

Way Forward

Plastic pollution disproportionately affects marginalized communities and communities living in close proximity to plastic production and waste sites, constituting an environmental injustice.[21] It is important to recognize these vulnerable groups and include them in local decision making.

To address the disproportionate impacts of plastics, there is a need to acknowledge and address societal roles in plastic pollution, reduce the risks, and hold producers accountable. Further, there is a need to encourage community-led initiatives and education, incentivize recycling scheme, just transition and re-skilling of waste pickers. Successful strategies must address the diverse and context-specific technological, social, political, ecological, and economic challenges in each place where they are implemented. Specifically, LMICs needs sustainable solutions, not more plastics. Protecting the environment, health, cultural heritage, and economy of LMICs would require supporting local entrepreneurs to develop sustainable alternatives to plastics.

Adetoun Mustapha Olaitan is a leading Environmental Epidemiologist in Africa. Her research is focused on air pollution, social determinants of

---

[20] See Adwoa Coleman, "Water Sachet Packaging Found a Recycle Source in West African Country: Nigeria Needed a Readily Available, Affordable Access to Potable Water," December 15, 2020, www.packagingstrategies.com/articles/95812-water-sachet-packaging-found-a-recycle-source-in-west-african-country; Kumar, et al., "Challenges and Opportunities Associated with Waste Management in India."

[21] See Juliano Calil, Marce Gutiérrez-Graudiņš, Azul Steffanie Munguía, and Christopher Chin, *Neglected: Environmental Justice Impacts of Marine Litter and Plastic Pollution* (United Nations Environment Programme, 2021).

health, plastic pollution, climate change and ethics. Her thrirty-year career spans industry, academia, and research. She is an adjunct Associate Professor of Environmental Epidemiology at the Lead City University, Nigeria and an adjunct Researcher at the Nigerian Institute of Medical Research (NIMR). She has been the Principal and Co-Principal Investigator in various impactful projects including the Population-Based Interventions towards Reducing the burden of Hypertension in Nigeria (PoBIRH), the Lagos Air Quality Monitoring Program, and the Nigerian Environmental Epidemiology Accelerated Research (NEEAR) Program. She has been an expert reviewer and member of various international groups such as the *Lancet* Commission on Pollution and Health, the Minderoo-Monaco Commission on Plastics and Human Health, and the World Health Organization Personal Interventions and Risk Communication on Air Pollution. She is a Fellow of the Collegium Ramazzini, Fellow of the International Society for Environmental Epidemiology (ISEE), the inaugural chair of International Society for Environmental Epidemiology (ISEE) Africa chapter and past Councilor for Africa in the ISEE Council. She is a recipient of several national and international awards including the ISEE Rebecca James Baker Memorial Prize.

4. Plastics and Inclusive Wealth

Pushpam Kumar

The Dangers of Plastics

Global plastic production has increased exponentially since the 1950s, reaching about 460 million tonnes in 2019.[1] The continuing growth of the global annual production of primary plastic is currently on course to possibly reaching 1.1 billion tonnes in 2050. Single-use plastics now comprise about forty percent of global plastic production.

Chemicals are an integral part of plastics.[2] Over sixteen thousand substances have so far been associated with plastics, either known for use in plastic production or detected in plastic materials. In addition to certain monomers, ten groups of chemicals (based on chemistry, uses, or sources) are identified as being of major concern due to their high toxicity and potential to migrate and/or be released from plastics, including specific flame retardants, certain UV stabilizers, per- and polyfluoroalkyl substances (PFASs), phthalates, bisphenols, alkylphenols and alkylphenol ethoxylates, biocides, certain metals and metalloids, polycyclic aromatic hydrocarbons, and many other non-intentionally added substances (NIAS).

Chemicals of concern have been found in plastics across a wide range of sectors and product value chains, including toys and other children's

---

[1] See Philip J. Landrigan, Hervé Raps, Maureen Cropper, Caroline Bald, Manuel Brunner, Elvia Maya Canonizado, et al., "The Minderoo-Monaco Commission on Plastics and Human Health," *Annals of Global Health* 89, no. 1 (2023), doi.org/10.5334/aogh.4056.

[2] See Martin Wagner, Laura Monclús, Hans Peter H. Arp, Ksenia J. Groh, Mari E. Løseth, Jane Muncke, Zhanyun Wang, Raoul Wolf, and Lisa Zimmermann, *State of the Science on Plastic Chemicals: Identifying and Addressing Chemicals and Polymers of Concern* (2024), zenodo.org/records/10701706.

products, packaging (including food contact materials), electrical and electronic equipment, vehicles, synthetic textiles and related materials, furniture, building materials, medical devices, personal care and household products, and agriculture, aquaculture, and fisheries.

Chemicals of concern in plastics can impact human health and the environment. Extensive scientific data on the potential adverse impacts of about seven thousand substances associated with plastics show that more than 3,200 of them have one or more hazardous properties of concern. These include chemicals that are persistent and mobile in the environment, accumulate in the body, can mimic, block or alter the actions of hormones, reduce fertility, damage the nervous system, and/or cause cancer.[3]

The Global Framework on Chemicals, adopted in Bonn (Germany) in October 2023, affirms the need and vision to move towards a pollution-free world.[4] It specifically "Invites relevant participating organizations of the Inter-Organization Programme for the Sound Management of Chemicals to update the existing costs of inaction report, taking into account quality-assured new research and the latest information relating to economic and social costs of unsound management of chemicals and waste at the national, regional and international levels."[5] Likewise, the Pact for the Future adopted in the seventy-ninth session of the UN General

---

[3] See United Nations Environment Programme (UNEP), and Secretariat of the Basel, Rotterdam, and Stockholm Conventions, "Chemicals in Plastics: A Technical Report" (2023), www.unep.org/resources/report/chemicals-plastics-technical-report.
[4] See United Nations Environment Programme, "Global Framework on Chemicals," www.chemicalsframework.org/.
[5] United Nations Environment Programme, "The Global Framework on Chemicals Resolutions," (2024), https://www.chemicalsframework.org/page/resolution-v3-financial-considerations. The quote is from: "Resolution V/3: Financial Considerations," no. 4. See also Mateo Cordier, Takuro Uehara, Bethany Jorgensen, and Juan Baztan, "Reducing Plastic Production: Economic Loss or Environmental Gain?," *Cambridge Prisms: Plastics* 2 (2024): e2, doi.org/10.1017/plc.2024.3; World Health Organization, Inter-Organization for the Sound Management of Chemicals (IOMC), "Working Together to End Plastic Pollution," partnership.who.int/iomc.

Assembly in New York clearly recommends integration of planetary and human health with explicit focus on integration of nature with finance for poverty alleviation and inequality reduction.[6]

Need for Better Economic Metrics

The existing global financial architecture—based mainly on Gross Domestic Product (GDP)—is not an adequate metric of the wealth of nations. It fails to measure plastics' harms to human and natural capital. Continued acceleration of growth and employment while not harming human health, strip-mining the planet's resources, or widening inequities will require that we reform our accounting systems and develop new macroeconomic metric that measure human and natural capital in addition to GDP. An example is seen in the Global Biodiversity Framework of the Convention on Biological Diversity, which emphasizes mainstreaming biodiversity into finance.[7]

To overcome the problems confronting the world within the triple planetary crisis—i.e., climate change, biodiversity loss, and pollution—it is essential that the world change how it views development and how it measures the wealth of nations. By using measures of Inclusive Wealth, society will be better equipped to track whether nations are making true progress. There is a growing consensus on the need to move beyond GDP to measure progress and sustainability.[8]

---

[6] See Vibhu Mishra, "Pact for the Future: World Leaders Pledge Action for Peace, Sustainable Development," *United Nations, UN News: Global Perspective Human Stories*, September 22, 2024, news.un.org/en/story/2024/09/1154671.

[7] See UN Convention on Biological Diversity, "Kunming-Montreal Global Biodiversity Framework," January 10, 2024, www.cbd.int/gbf.

[8] See United Nations Systems, Chief Executives Board for Coordination (CEB), "Valuing What Counts: United Nations System-wide Contribution on Progress Beyond Gross Domestic Product (GDP)," August 17, 2022, unsceb.org/valuing-what-counts-united-nations-system-wide-contribution-beyond-gross-domestic-product-gdp.

While GDP provides important information on the flow aspects of the national accounts, the stock part (i.e., the world's stocks of natural assets, which include geology, soil, air, water and all living things), especially natural capital, remains outside the domain of transaction and accounting and is not measured by GDP. Defining stocks, quantifying them, and internalizing them into the National Accounts System would keep track of sustainability. In this context assessing both the human wealth produced and the natural wealth in inclusive ways, and avoiding over-reliance on market price or GDP, would provide a more realistic picture of how we are addressing the environment and impact of economic activities.

The Inclusive Wealth Index

The Inclusive Wealth Index (IWI) is a metric developed by the United Nations Environment Programme (UNEP) in response to the Beyond GDP movement. The Inclusive Wealth Index measures the assets that underpin a nation's income flows and human well-being: natural, human, and produced capital. Measuring inclusive wealth is key to driving sustainable investments across all policy areas. The sum of natural assets plus human and produced assets determine an economy's Inclusive Wealth and are the building blocks for achieving the Sustainable Development Goals (SDGs).[9]

The Inclusive Wealth Index measures the wealth of nations by conducting a comprehensive analysis of a country's productive base, including the assets from which human well-being is derived, as well as those manufactured, and human and natural capital. Thus, IWI measures a nation's capacity to create and maintain human well-being over time.[10]

The UNEP Inclusive Wealth Report 2023 undertook a comprehensive global assessment of the inclusive wealth of 163 countries between 1992

---

[9] See United Nations, Department of Economic and Social Affairs, "The 17 Goals," sdgs.un.org/goals.
[10] See United Nations Environment Programme, *Inclusive Wealth 2023: Measuring Sustainability and Equity* (2023), doi.org/10.59117/20.500.11822/43131.

and 2019.[11] The Inclusive Wealth Index can supplement GDP to capture a comprehensive assessment of economy-environment interactions. Individual countries like USA, Canada, Australia, UK, Kenya, Ethiopia, Indonesia, and others have already started working on it. The Inclusive Wealth Report highlights how inclusive wealth—incorporating natural, human, and produced capital—is a sophisticated yet streamlined measure for assessing national and global development and economic progress.

As noted by the Dasgupta Report, *The Economics of Biodiversity*, judging "whether the path of economic development . . . is sustainable" requires nations to adopt "inclusive measure[s] of their wealth."[12] Likewise, the United States White House Office of Science and Technology Policy has clearly articulated needs for natural capital assets accounts.[13] The World Bank,[14] the Organisation for Economic Co-operation and Development (OECD),[15] and the World Economic Forum[16] agree that decision-makers must focus on increasing wealth and reducing economic inequity if they want to ensure well-being in the twenty-first century.

Rising GDP per capita is linked to higher rates of poverty and inequality within nations. Relying solely on GDP growth for policy formulation does not effectively address poverty and inequality.[17] The IWI

---

[11] See United Nations Environment Programme, *Inclusive Wealth 2023*.

[12] Partha Dasgupta, *The Economics of Biodiversity: The Dasgupta Review* (HM Treasury, 2021), 5.

[13] See White House, "Office of Science and Technology Policy," bidenwhitehouse.archives.gov/ostp/.

[14] See World Bank, *The Changing Wealth of Nations 2021: Managing Assets for the Future* (World Bank, 2021), hdl.handle.net/10986/36400.

[15] See Organisation for Economic Cooperation and Development (OECD), *Inequalities in Household Wealth and Financial Insecurity of Households* (2021), www.oecd.org/content/dam/oecd/en/publications/reports/2021/07/inequalities-in-household-wealth-and-financial-insecurity-of-households_f2d465bb/b60226a0-en.pdf

[16] See World Economic Forum, *The Inclusive Development Index 2018* (2018), weforum.org/publications/the-inclusive-development-index-2018/.

[17] See Organisation for Economic Cooperation and Development (OECD), *Inequalities in Household Wealth and Financial Insecurity of Households*.

provides a more holistic economic assessment, particularly important for low-income countries which are often most vulnerable to the impacts of natural capital depletion.[18] IWI would also capture how plastics and chemicals are affecting human capital in the economy through causing increased mortality and morbidity and thus impeding the formation of human capital. Use of the IWI will help the economy and society to track progress toward meeting the Sustainable Development Goals, reduce inequity, and safeguard human health.

Pushpam Kumar is Chief Environmental Economist and Senior Economic Advisor of the UN Environment Program (UNEP), where he leads various initiatives. He has been instrumental in designing, implementing, and providing leadership to the concept of Natural Capital through flagship projects like VANTAGE (Valuation and Accounting of Natural Capital for Green Economy) and Proecoserv, culminating in a resolution on Natural Capital passed during UNEA2 in 2016. He served as member of the Expert Panel of the National Ecosystem Assessment (NEA) and of the Gulbenkia Ocean Initiative Advisory Board (Lisbon). He was closely associated with the 2007 Nobel Peace Prize of the Intergovernmental Panel on Climate Change (IPCC). He was co-coordinating lead author of the Responses Working Group of the Millennium Ecosystem Assessment. He also co-chaired the World Bank Policy and Technical Committee of the Wealth Accounting and Valuation of Ecosystem Services (WAVES) Programme. He has a PhD in Environmental Economics and, in 1991–2010, he was at the University of Liverpool and University of Delhi as Associate Professor and Professor in Environmental Economics. He is Honorary Research Scientist at the Earth Institute of Columbia University (New York) and is an Extra-

---

[18] See UN Environment Programme, *Inclusive Wealth for Africa 2024*: *Moving Beyond GDP* (2024), wedocs.unep.org/xmlui/handle/20.500.11822/43651.

Ordinary Professor at the University of Pretoria. He has widely published in peer-reviewed journals and authored or edited more than eight books. He has been board member of the International Society for Ecological Economics, Indian Society for Ecological Economics, and European Society for Ecological Economics. He is also on the editorial board of various journals including *Ecological Economics*.

Part 3

Responding Ethically

5. Becoming Plastic, Transforming Justice

Willis Jenkins

In early Christian thought, the word "plastic" often referred to the human being. From the Greek verb *plassō* for molding and making, emerged a word for the quality of being able to be molded: *plastikos*—the quality of being formable by the intent of another. In Romans 9:20, Paul works with root words of *plassō* to describe the human being as *to plasma,* the one formed, in relation to God, the one who forms us. Theologians like Irenaeus (born in 130) and Gregory of Nyssa (†394) used the term to describe human transformability. Being plastic, in that sense, was a central characteristic of being human, a sense that continued through Romanticism, as in the phrase "the one Spirit's plastic stress" of Percy Bysshe Shelley (1792–1822) in his poem "Adonais," which influences words of Gerard Manley Hopkins (1844–1899) "instress" and "inscape" to explore how God works on humans through created beauty.[1] In other words, from the New Testament into the nineteenth century, a primary referent for "plastic" in Christian theology was the human interior, transformable before the creativity of God.

After the twentieth century the word now means nearly the reverse: a human product whose quality is its moldability to our will. And, in tragic irony, this substance made by human transformative powers has become name of a scourge, a pervasive blight that itself seems to be altering lifeworlds, to the extent that some suggest plastic will become the signature geological evidence of an epoch of irresponsible anthropogenic influence: the plasticene.[2] It has become a name for the Anthropocene because plastic

---

[1] See W.H. Gardner's introduction to Gerard Manley Hopkins, *Poems and Prose* (Penguin Classics, 1985), xx–xxv.
[2] See Christina Reed, "Dawn of the Plasticene Age," *New Scientist* 225, no. 3006 (2015): 28–32.

exemplifies its paradoxes: a planet remade by powerful humans in their own image becomes, by the substance of those very powers, increasingly inhospitable to them.

As with other drivers of adverse planetary changes, some resistance to interventions may be rooted in a sense that technological societies cannot change, that plastics are more or less inevitable because the human drive for material progress and expansion of power is fixed in human nature. Sometimes that sense of inevitability is glossed with the view that good societies accept such negative trade-offs from a fundamental commitment to freedom, which over the long run increases human welfare. That the vulnerable disproportionately bear the burden of those trade-offs may be seen as unfortunate but acceptable for building wealth and power for humanity. Necessary to the work of building responsibilities for plastic pollution, climate disruption, and species extinctions is countering that combination of technological fatalism, free market fundamentalism, and indifference to justice by recovering the view that humans can be transformed.

Perhaps an indication of the depth of our troubles, moral and cultural transformation has emerged as a theme in global institutions tracking planetary problems. The Intergovernmental Panel on Climate Change (IPCC) now goes beyond its previous calls for transitions in material systems to summon "long-term transformation" in social systems "including altered goals or values."[3] In its most recent assessment report Intergovernmental Panel on Biodiversity and Ecosystem Services (IPBES) calls for "transformative change" across sectors, which it specifies as "fundamental, system-wide reorganization across technological, economic and social factors, *including paradigms, goals, and values.*"[4] While seemingly naïve to the brittle fixities of modern assumptions about human

---

[3] Intergovernmental Panel on Climate Change (IPCC), Working Group II, *Climate Change 2022: Impacts, Adaptation, and Vulnerability* (2022), www.ipcc.ch/report/ar6/wg2/.

[4] Intergovernmental Science-Policy Platform on Biodiversity and Ecosystem Services (IPBES), "Summary for Policymakers," *Global Assessment Report on Biodiversity and Ecosystem Services* (2019), www.ipbes.net/global-assessment. Italic in original.

nature and economic organization, that transformability of values is something to which Christian theology has long attested: we are actually made for great transitions.

The early Christian uses of plasticity hold out hope that our values, practices, institutions, traditions, and maybe even our senses of what it is to be human can be remolded. Human transformability was an important condition for thinking about faithfulness, which included entrusting oneself to be molded by God into responsibility for all one's relations. So one pattern of answer to the problem of pervasive plastics pollution is that we must, in a sense, become more plastic.

Six Ways to Make Polymers into Problems

Central to the work of transition is making everyday materials into moral problems. How does a mundane, throw-away substance become a moral problem? When challenges involve relations unfamiliar to the inheritances by which people make sense of their world, or which seem outside the repertoire of virtues and obligations through which a tradition forms persons, then a key task for ethics is to extend interpretive and practical competencies.[5] For example, until the mid-twentieth century, the atmosphere was not usually a domain of moral responsibility and fossil fuel energy was benignly irrelevant to ethics. With the ebullition of anthropogenic climate change, a major project for ethics within and across moral worlds focuses on catalyzing processes by which previously benign substances and planetary relations become significant for how people and institutions understand their responsibilities and perhaps their sense of personhood.

I here sketch six approaches for turning polymers and their impacts into redressable moral problems. Each of the six may be assessed for their adequacy to the challenge, yet it is important to note that their liabilities

---

[5] See Willis Jenkins, *The Future of Ethics: Sustainability, Social Justice, and Religious Creativity* (Georgetown University Press, 2013).

and affordances differ within specific moral, religious, or political worlds where they catalyze responsibility. In some cases, preference for a specific approach to problematizing may be preferred by the moral world in which it has the most purchase. Each also leads to a different view of the tradeoffs involved. While the focus of assessment will be on an approach's potential to mitigate the manifold harms of global plastics pollution as summarized in the 2023 Minderoo-Monaco Commission on Plastics and Human Health, I take as a given that plastics are pervasive in part because they are convenient and efficient, associated with many quality of life improvements expanded to more of the human family than ever before. As just one example, the Minderoo-Monaco Report notes the role of disposable plastics in medical contexts for the control of infection. In that and other cases, substitutions are not always easy and may carry trade-offs that have their own impacts on distributive justice or care for the vulnerable.[6]

1. *Trash Containment*

Polymers may first attract notice as a problem of mismanaged trash, disturbing because of their pervasiveness and ugliness. Strewn on roadsides, lining riverbanks, mixed into agricultural fields, washing up on beaches, caught in the stomachs of marine animals—plastics constantly frustrate waste management strategies. Like "dirt" in Mary Douglas's account, "trash" is a social category, referring to matter that belongs in socially-approved disposal flows and seems threatening when encountered outside of them.[7] At low levels, the threat of mismanaged matter may be experienced as merely annoying but at high levels may be perceived as a threat to social organization or a sign of social disintegration, perhaps

---

[6] See Philip J. Landrigan, Hervé Raps, Maureen Cropper, Caroline Bald, Manuel Brunner, Elvia Maya Canonizado, et al., "The Minderoo-Monaco Commission on Plastics and Human Health," *Annals of Global Health* 89, no. 1 (2023): 1–215.

[7] See Mary Douglas, *Purity and Danger: An Analysis of Concepts of Pollution and Taboo* (Routledge, 1967).

because the category of trash, which contains disused matter, is overwhelmed by plastics, which seem uncontainable. Affective recoil from a trashscape can thus drive critical questions about what has gone wrong in social organization and what must change.

However, framing plastic pollution as a waste management problem can yield weak solutions and may be given to prejudice. It is weak when this framing suggests that the solution is not to have fewer or safer polymers enter global productions, but rather that what is needed is stronger containment of them at local levels. That perception can, in turn, feed prejudice by lending itself to judgement about the kinds of communities who have trouble managing their waste, and so to the long histories of in-group perceptions that their practices are cleaner than those of outsiders. Producers will generally welcome the release of responsibility in interpretations that move in this direction, as for example in scientific papers that track flows of plastic trash and find that they come disproportionately from certain demographics, or a particular region, or from poorer countries.[8] Socially-shaped perception of uncontained trash, in other words, may unfairly channel blame toward local failures of containment rather than Global North negligence in production.

On the other hand, aesthetic response to trash can point attention to human rights implications of locally mismanaged plastic waste. Inadequate waste management is often paired with and exacerbated by inadequate access to water and sanitation. When people do not have access to clean water, they may buy water in plastic bags;[9] when they do not have access to latrines they may use plastic bags; and without waste management, the disposed bags clog public drains and sewers, further degrading the habitability of a place. Plastic trash becomes a landscape of human degradation; in some places it becomes the ever-present medium of social and ecological relations for embodied human persons. In smoking

---

[8] See Jenna R. Jambeck, Roland Geyer, Chris Wilcox, Theodore R. Siegler, Miriam Perryman, Anthony Andrady, et al., "Plastic Waste Inputs from Land into the Ocean," *Science* 347, no. 6223 (2015): 768–771.

[9] See Adetoun Mustapha Olaitan's chapter in this volume.

mountains of plastic waste worked globally by millions of people sustaining themselves as trash-pickers, uncontained plastics significantly determine the world available to human residents.

2. *Bodily Contamination*

A second approach to making plastics into a moral problem focuses on violation of the sanctity of one's body. This approach is akin to the trash perception but is here intensified in relation to the special status of human bodies. The Minderoo-Monaco Report summarizes findings about the plastics increasingly found inside humans, as small particles enter through ingestion, inhalation, or absorption. They may pass through but sometimes travel within us, sometimes crossing into organs or circulating in blood. Even if the health impacts are uncertain, many people may feel repugnance or anger at unlicensed trespass of their body.

Sanctity violated or purity tainted can link to powerful moral responses. Jonathan Haidt argues that they matter especially to conservative moral systems.[10] While Haidt holds that such systems tend not to weigh harm and fairness as heavily as liberal frameworks, leading to relatively less concern regarding distributional harms of plastic trash, conservatives' emphasis on bodily purity and disgust at contamination may make them more likely to be outraged or frightened by discoveries of manufactured substances mixed into their blood.

A drawback to this approach for plastics lies in its susceptibility to being overwhelmed by their pervasive unavoidability. As Alexis Shotwell notes, like other Anthropocene problems, the overwhelm can generate a "purity politics of despair"; if the moral problem arises from obligations to separate oneself from unavoidably entangling relations, the result will quickly transition from outrage to resignation.[11] Plastic is everywhere and

---

[10] See Jonathan Haidt, *The Righteous Mind: Why Good People Are Divided by Politics and Religion* (Pantheon Books, 2012).

[11] Alexis Shotwell, *Against Purity: Living Ethically in Compromised Times* (University of Minnesota Press, 2016), 195.

will be for as long as we here are alive. Rather than despair at the impossibility of avoiding a monstrous substance, we need ways to develop collective responsibility for the mixed worlds we are making, to develop meaningful freedom with plastics.

3. *Violence and Injury*

The next three approaches correspond to harms described by the Minderoo-Monaco Report: plastics are injuring and killing humans; those already vulnerable are disproportionately exposed; and plastics are killing other creatures and damaging lifeworlds on which all of us depend. Much of the moral work here is accomplished by sheer description. Taking in the cumulative record of science-based research on the harms caused by plastics, one cannot but conclude that there are violations of human dignity and creaturely integrity, so I will briefly underscore three key findings related to injustice, before extending the scope of justice involved.

On the first major form of harm, the Minderoo-Monaco Report is unequivocal: "Plastic is responsible for [human] disease, disability, and premature death at every stage of its lifecycle."[12] From water pollution in extraction to airborne microfibers in manufacture to neurotoxin exposures in everyday use to carcinogens produced in waste management, a mass of evidence shows plastics harming human. Are those individual harms worth the aggregate benefits they produce? The cumulative cost of the health impacts in 2015 in the United States alone, including 91,000 premature deaths, the report estimates at $921 billion, or about five per cent of gross domestic product (GDP)—a figure that does not include the health impacts associated with related climate impacts. If we take the costs as an indicator of magnitude, it is not hard to conclude that we are all bearing avoidable harms created by an industrial process with insufficient guardrails and safety protocols.

---

[12] Landrigan, et al., "The Minderoo-Monaco Commission," 6.

4. Distributive Injustice

We are not all bearing those harms equally, however. That children are especially vulnerable points to a second dimension of justice: plastic harms disproportionately affect those already vulnerable. The Minderoo-Monaco Report documents how those harms follow and intensify historic injustices: "health consequences fall disproportionately on the poor, minorities, the marginalized and people in the Global South."[13] From fenceline neighborhoods near production facilities, to the dangerous packaging for inexpensive goods needed in poorer communities, to the burdens of waste and pollution, negative consequences of plastic are pushed by social power into the backyards and bodies of the disempowered. In other words, the affluent take advantage of inequalities to ensure that the greater burden of harms fall on those minoritized, impoverished, or otherwise excluded. That is in itself an injustice.

Repair requires redressing aspects of procedural injustice, which begins with adequate stakeholder participation in decision-making processes. That includes a right to meaningful information about risks and benefits, which entails a right to intelligible science linked to the best available knowledge about health outcomes. Procedural justice is relevant at every scale in which the problem is experienced, so while it includes stakeholder participation in decisions about where to locate production and waste facilities, it goes beyond that to democratize deliberations over how much and what kinds of plastic production make sense. And because unjust distribution of harms from plastics follows global inequalities, especially in the flow of waste from Global North to Global South, procedural justice requires representation from all the relations involved in the plastic lifecycle.

Procedural justice in implementing policy change is also critical because, as the history of environmental justice movements attests, the burden of environmental intervention also tends to be born more heavily

---

[13] Landrigan, et al., "The Minderoo-Monaco Commission," 103.

by the vulnerable. Plastics are associated with many quality-of-life improvements that matter especially to the vulnerable, like transporting potable water where it is unavailable or the role of disposable plastics in medical contexts for the control of infection. In these and other cases, substitutions are not always easy and may carry trade-offs that have their own impacts on distributive justice or care for the vulnerable. Just as burdens of the problem fall more heavily on the vulnerable, so can policy interventions if not designed with their interests and voices. Governance processes will be more fair when weighted so that there is more voice and priority for those populations most impacted by plastics.

5. *Multispecies Injustice*

A harm-focused approach to making plastics into a moral problem involves non-human creatures and living systems. Of course, many of these harms also indirectly affect human health and so would be mitigated by better human public health protections, but there is another, distinct kind of justice issue here. Insofar as coral reefs or marine mammals have their own integrity or dignity or value or right—to use four terms offered by Pope Francis over recent years—then avoidable harm to other creatures and their worlds is its own injustice. The Minderoo-Monaco Report reviews the state of scientific knowledge on vulnerabilities to non-human animals and living systems, about which there are many uncertainties and gaps in knowledge. Yet enough is known for a global treaty to recognize three distinct levels of injustice.

The first is negligent injury to other individual organisms, as in the entanglement of sea turtles in plastic lines or ingestion of plastics as mistaken food. The second is extinction pressure on species and communities, as in the additional stress microplastics seem to create for coral reefs, already under pressure from warming waters, or correlations of plastic ingestion with failed seabird nests. Because extinction shuts down evolutionary possibilities of adaptation it might also be considered a kind of procedural injustice, excluding more-than-human forms of responsibility for a world with plastics. Finally, there is the issue of disrespectful relations with fellow creatures; whatever the impacts, the relations themselves are characterized by absence of moral recognition, which is itself an injustice. For example, releasing toxic materials that in appearance, smell, or chemical signature present as food to other animals seems disrespectful as an act.

6. *Colonial Injustice, Integrative Repair*

The previous three harm-focused approaches to making polymers into problems overlap but they do not always integrate. The different kinds and lenses of justice they involve seem different. Concern to protect my own body from toxic trespass may lead to policy interventions with consequences disproportionately borne by the vulnerable; meanwhile, prioritizing the human vulnerable might require sacrificing regard for non-humans. These different lenses of justice, when overlaid, may seem to blur our moral vision.

Consider anew the example of plastics that look like food to other creatures to illustrate how harms to non-human creatures may connect to structures of violence and injustice to other humans. Non-compostable materials are disrespectful because they cannot feed other creatures. In the case of a single-use disposable straw the temporalities are especially mismatched: a ten-second use of a material with a thousand-year life. That kind of plastic use carries a colonial premise: that land and water can be used to store the long-term consequences of societies built to support pursuit of short-term interest.

On this approach, confronting plastics pollution is an opportunity to confront colonial premises and repair divided senses of justice—including the idea that land exists for human benefit and that "human benefit" is determined by the perceived needs of dominant societies. In the book *Pollution as Colonialism*, plastics researcher Max Liboiron argues that the conventional model for assessing pollution "is based on land relations that strip away the complexities of Land—including relations to fish, spirits, humans, water, and other entities—in favor of elements relevant to settler and colonial goals for using the water as a sink, a site of storage for waste."[14]

The pursuit of human benefit has often justified colonial forms of extraction, production, and waste, with the (sometimes silent, sometimes explicit) view that not all humans are included in the humanity who benefits. When adverse outcomes—like climate disruption or plastics pollution—are treated as contemporary pan-human imperatives to avoid looming catastrophes of the future, it can de-historicize them, deflecting attention away from the histories of injustice from which they are produced.[15] Separated from their histories, the different trajectories of injustice seem separate and rivalrous. Just so, making plastics a problem of colonial injustice may reintegrate accounts of justice. Liboiron writes, "Plastics are an ideal pollutant to upset dominant norms of pollution [because]... their industrial, intergenerational, and ubiquitous relations make a lot of room for understanding and doing things differently."[16]

Procedural justice offers a way to start that work of reintegrating and repairing. In a review of published work on plastics, Liboiron and Cotter find that "sources authored by Indigenous individuals or organizations were more likely to directly oppose colonial systems of pollution in favor of rights- and justice-based modes of governance."[17] For another example, the involvement of waste pickers as knowledge holders has expanded the ambitions of justice in the effort toward a UN treaty on plastics.[18] So, while

---

[14] Max Liboiron, *Pollution Is Colonialism* (Duke University Press, 2021), 40.

[15] See Nelly Wamaitha, "The False Promise of Progress," *Journal of the Society of Christian Ethics* 41, no. 2 (2021): 297–314.

[16] Liboiron, *Pollution Is Colonialism*, 101.

[17] Max Liboiron and Riley Cotter, "Review of Participation of Indigenous Peoples in Plastics Pollution Governance," *Cambridge Prisms: Plastics* 1 (2023): e16, 1–16, doi.org/10.1017/plc.2023.16.

[18] See Patrick O'Hare and Emmy Nøklebye, "'The Human Face of the UN Plastics Treaty'? The Role of Waste Pickers in Intergovernmental Negotiations to End Plastic Pollution and Ensure a Just Transition," *Cambridge Prisms: Plastics* 2 (2024): e12, 1–12, doi.org/10.1017/plc.2024.12. In this volume, see also Adetoun Mustapha Olaitan's chapter.

divisions in inherited ideas of justice may be under pressure from the scale and complexity of relations involved with plastics, combined with inequality among humans, there is evidence that democratizing deliberation expands the range of what justice can do. Especially when it reckons with an inherited world shaped by colonialism, reparative justice may become more integrative and ambitious. Thus, Olufemi Taiwo writes: "If slavery and colonialism built the world and its current basic scheme of social injustice, the proper task of social justice is no smaller: it is, quite literally, to remake the world."[19]

Conclusion: Five Tactics

Olúfẹ́mi O. Táíwò observes that worldmaking does not need a comprehensive plan to get started; transformative responsibilities are more likely to develop from pluralist experimentation with multiple tactics. We do not need a comprehensive solution so much as to see truthfully what we inherit and invent ways to reshape those inheritances and what they have made of us.[20] The following five tactics represent ways to exercise plasticity: the capacity for humans and their social forms to reshape themselves in response to challenges.

Cap Production

An important condition for repair and transformation is time. Plastics have been under commercial production just a bit longer than the average lifespan of an albatross, about as long as a human life, since about the signing of the 1948 "Universal Declaration of Human Rights."[21] It makes sense, then, that ecological and cultural systems would find it difficult to

---

[19] Olúfẹ́mi O. Táíwò, *Reconsidering Reparations* (Oxford University Press, 2022), 67.
[20] See Táíwò, *Reconsidering Reparations*, chapters 5–6.
[21] See United Nations, "Universal Declaration of Human Rights" (1948), www.un.org/en/about-us/universal-declaration-of-human-rights.

adapt quickly enough. But that can also be reason for hope: slow down production to give cultural and ecological systems time to make sense of this transforming substance, to accommodate it. A global treaty capping production is not simply about slowing a waste stream; it is about expanding time for all creatures to understand and accommodate plastic ways of being. Caps should thus focus on the most dangerous polymers devoted to the most transient uses.

Inclusive Science

A global treaty should authorize ongoing science-based work to establish thresholds for minimum protection of rights to a reasonably safe environment, beginning with the air we breathe and water we drink, benchmarked from humans who are most vulnerable. That will require ongoing evidence-based research which itself will require more transparent disclosure and public sharing of information, which is key for making our moral tools, from purity to welfarism to rights, more competent to plastics. At the same time, a permanent scientific consultative body will be more representative and effective if includes ways of knowing investigated in humanities and social sciences—something the IPCC and IPBES discovered late and have in recent year been working to incorporate. That includes work from Indigenous knowledge, religious traditions, ethical frameworks, and/or cultural values. Plastics science should be a democratizing practice in itself, something to which many can contribute, including through community-led approaches. There is an element of epistemic justice here, and it also may be tactically advantageous for a diversified, inclusive, pluralist approach to making expert knowledge.

Extended Producer Responsibility

By treaty, policy, or tort, we must create ways to hold plastics producers legally and financially responsible for the safety of their products over their full lifecycle. That would shift responsibility for safety and pollution management from governments and individuals wrestling with this uncontainable substance imposed into our common life, to the institutions who make them. A polluter-pays model would incentivize safer manufacturing processes, more prudent quantities, more innovative development to meet related needs, and investment in adequate waste systems everywhere the product goes. Where policy fails, litigation might establish criminal negligence or public nuisance. Where there is evidence that specific producers had knowledge that their products cause harm and that it could not be contained by existing waste management (as California has accused Exxon),[22] producer responsibility extends to the costs of intentionally frustrating the cultural and political processes through which societies develop responsibilities for new problems. That is an injustice in itself and one for which companies involved owe reparations, which should not only be monetary damages but apology and truth-telling.

Rights of Rivers and Oceans

Rights for nature are recognized in a number of jurisdictions, often due to successful political and legal strategies from Indigenous Peoples organizations. They have been especially successful in regard to rivers, which ostensibly can now sue polluters should their functions be impinged. While there are many practical and jurisprudential questions around these kinds of rights, consider what the effort to answer them might do for this problem. If every major river had legal standing in its watershed, such that pollution represented a direct infringement and remedies pursued directly benefitted the river, waterways could not be regarded as mere waste conduits. For societies in which it is unusual, inventing ways to regard rivers as legal and moral persons to whom we are accountable may be a kind of anti-colonial cultural tonic, upsetting the

---

[22] See Lisa Song, "ExxonMobil Accused of 'Deceptively' Promoting Chemical Recycling as a Solution for the Plastics Crisis," *ProPublica*, September 27, 2024, www.propublica.org/article/exxonmobil-plastics-recycling-pyrolysis-lawsuit-california. In this book, see also Judith Enck's chapter.

common sense that rivers are resources and conveniences for sending plastic trash to those ancient beings, the oceans.

Good Life with Plastic

Confronting plastics, like confronting climate disruption and extinctions, involves thinking about how to live good lives in troublesome unsolvable relations. Some cultural responses think it impossible and look to colonize Mars—a telling impulse, damned in its premise. But among many counter examples, consider the *Buen Vivir* movement reclaiming and inventing ways of living well that do not depend on post-colonial modernization. When linked to political affiliations, that kind of work can begin as small as a food co-op with minimal plastics. There is meaningful work to do in reclaiming patterns of a good life that do not depend on, and are less constrained by, the polymer supplement created by fossil fuel extraction. As the Minderoo-Monaco Report notes, half of all plastic ever produced was made after 2002, which suggests that reinventing social forms that do not depend so extensively on plastic should not take a massive effort in cultural memory. A flourishing human life does not require so much plastic, although it may take intentional work to recover our own plasticity, our transformability by the goodness of creation.

Willis Jenkins, PhD, lives in the Rivanna River watershed (Monacan land), where he works as Hollingsworth Professor of Ethics and Chair of the Department of Religious Studies at the University of Virginia. He is author of two award-winning books: *Ecologies of Grace: Environmental Ethics and Christian Theology*, which won a Templeton Award for Theological Promise, and *The Future of Ethics: Sustainability, Social Justice, and Religious Creativity*, which won an American Academy of Religion Award for Excellence. He is co-editor of several books, including the *Routledge Handbook of Religion and Ecology*, and many essays along intersections of religion, ethics, and environmental humanities. He co-directs the Coastal Futures Conservatory, which integrates arts and humanities into coastal change research at the National Science Foundation's Virginia Coast Reserve Long-Term Ecological Research site.

6. Plastics, Markets, and the Preferential Option for the Poor: What Can Be Done, and by Whom?

Christina G. McRorie

As a Catholic theological ethicist whose primary area of research is markets and economics, my focus in this chapter is on plastics as an economic question, seen in light of the principle of the preferential option for the poor. How, this chapter asks, does this principle recast the problem of plastics—and what does it suggest should and can be done about it, by whom?

The Preferential Option for the Poor

The preferential option is a principle that sits at the heart of Christian ethics in general, and Catholic social thought (CST) in particular. The name itself can be confusing, not least because "preference" and "option" make it seem elective. However, this principle is meant to be anything but. While in English the word option tends to imply that we are free to make a choice (or not), this theological term comes from conversations about the necessity of making a fundamental choice, as when the person chooses for God and goodness. This principle declares that we must individually and collectively decide to center the needs of the poor—and that we must do so preferentially, giving them priority.

Within Catholic ethics, this principle has been articulated in these precise terms only in the twentieth century. But the concept itself has its roots originally in Scripture, which consistently depicts God as having a special regard for the well-being of the most vulnerable. In the Hebrew scriptures, the covenantal instruction to care for the widow, the orphan, and the sojourner were usually paired with reminders of the ways that God had protected Israel in its own times of need. This underscored that the command to care for the vulnerable was not a minor or secondary obligation but central to what it meant for Israel to become God's people and to imitate and take on God's own righteousness.

We see this norm intensified further in the New Testament, when the Gospel of Matthew records Jesus as identifying *with* the poor, when he declares that the key criteria distinguishing his true followers will be whether they have fed the hungry, clothed the naked, cared for the sick, and so forth—because their actions toward "the least of these" will ultimately have been directed toward Christ himself.[1] With this in mind, the Catholic ethicist MT Dávila has described the preferential option as an "incarnational principle," because it invites us to participate in Christ's own character by actively prioritizing the welfare of those who are suffering, excluded, and powerless.[2]

Finally, in more recent years, this has been further nuanced with the caveat that this principle cannot merely be an imperative to serve the marginalized by meeting their needs *for* them, but that this must also include empowering *their* agency. This keeps this principle from becoming paternalistic and mere charity: to truly have an enduring commitment to the dignity of the most vulnerable means acting to empower them as agents in their own lives and following their lead when it comes to solving problems that affect them.

On one level, the application of this principle to the problem of plastics is clear: something is wrong with the way humans are currently producing, using, and disposing of plastics, not only because the harms overall are immense and climbing, but because these are disproportionately visited upon the "least of these." I obviously take this latter point to be firmly established, not least by the Minderoo-Monaco report: it seems

---

[1] Matthew 25: 31–46, NRSVCE. In this, Jesus tells his followers, "Truly I tell you, just as you did it to one of the least of these who are members of my family, you did it to me," and in turn, "just as you did not do it to one of the least of these, you did not do it to me."

[2] MT Dávila, "The Role of the Social Sciences in Catholic Social Thought: The Incarnational Nature of the Option for the Poor and Being Able to 'See' in the Rubric 'See, Judge, Act,'" *Journal of Catholic Social Thought* 9, no. 2 (2012): 232.

undeniable now that the destructive consequences of our overuse of plastics are many, and that they are distributed unequally, with the heaviest burdens borne by those with least power and privilege.[3] For those who agree with this empirical claim and who share the moral priority of preferentially caring for the poor, our current trajectory of using plastics appears a significant injustice that cries out for redress.

But of course, it is no good to simply denounce the evils of the status quo; ethics must be able to say much more than this. What can we say about what can be done, moving forward? Who has the capacity—and thus the responsibility—to preferentially address the needs of the poor, when it comes to plastics?

One Tempting (but 2-D) Reading of the Crisis: Fatalism about Markets Producing the Problem

For many in the humanities, both the scale and the deeply economic nature of this crisis make it hard to know how to tackle such questions. By pointing to the global economic shifts behind the recent increase in plastics production, the Minderoo-Monaco report underscores the immense profitability of the industry overall and the strong financial incentives that drive plastics production and usage.[4] Contemplating this situation, it can be tempting to draw two conclusions. The first is that markets themselves are a big part of the problem, if not *the* core cause: it is markets doing what they do—i.e., chasing profit—that has gotten us here. And secondly, if markets are the real cause of the crisis, this suggests that any solution will need to come from "outside" them, by forcibly curbing this relentless pursuit of profit. In this view, perhaps the preferential option should have been the responsibility of big business—both plastics producers and

---

[3] See Philip J. Landrigan, Hervé Raps, Maureen Cropper, Caroline Bald, Manuel Brunner, Elvia Maya Canonizado, et al., "The Minderoo-Monaco Commission on Plastics and Human Health," *Annals of Global Health* 89, no. 1 (2023): 103–114.
[4] See Landrigan, et al., "The Minderoo-Monaco Commission," 2.

producers of the fossil fuels used to make them—but because these parties will not act to change, it will be the responsibility of government to intervene in markets and compel them to do the right thing, at great cost.

This framing of the crisis is not a very hopeful one. To start with, it suggests that real change is not likely, given that mobilizing the transnational political necessary to oppose profitable sectors of the global economy will be no minor thing. By this same token, this approach paints those who want a dramatically different future as idealistic and perhaps even naïve. But perhaps most significantly, this way of thinking does not leave anyone else—that is, anyone who is not a CEO or in a position to promulgate important legislation—with much agency vis-à-vis the crisis. This largely leaves the rest of us sitting around, waiting for those in charge to make the necessary changes and finally exercise an option for the poor.

There is a certain amount of grim truth to this picture. Market incentives being what they are, "top-down" actions to restrict certain forms of business in the plastics industry will be an utterly indispensable part of any real way forward in addressing the escalating harms caused by current patterns of plastics production and disposal.

That said, I would like to suggest that this is not the *whole* picture; instead, it is more of a two-dimensional rendering of our situation—accurate in key respects but also incomplete. Above all, this narration relies on an overly-simplistic picture of how markets work, by presuming that they work only one way. As a result, such a view suggests an unnecessarily limited picture of what can be done about economic injustices and by whom. Against this view, I suggest that CST and economics offer complementary resources that can help us see the plastics crisis in more three-dimensional terms—that is, as one that takes place in markets, to be sure, but is simultaneously social, cultural, political, technological, and even spiritual in nature. This broader perspective on the crisis can accordingly widen our thinking about who is called to address it by implementing the preferential option for the poor.

How CST and Economics Can Help Us See It in 3-D

Let me begin with the normative worldview of CST. The tradition of CST has long refused to conceptually separate something called "the economic" from something else called "the social."[5] No matter how convenient it is to use these terms to describe different dimensions of social life, CST invites us to remember that in reality, these are not actually isolable domains, because we are ultimately integrated beings. Remembering this reality requires rejecting fatalistic thinking about what goes on in "the economy," as if it were an utterly autonomous and a-social realm governed by its own immutable laws and thus exempt from the moral norms that apply in other areas of social life. Instead of buying into that kind of dichotomous thinking, CST urges us to consider how the economic, political, and even spiritual dimensions of the social challenges that we face are all interconnected—and, moreover, how the values of the Gospel speak to each. Because this, finally, is the ethical takeaway of adopting an integrated worldview: the conviction that the Gospel applies to *all* of social life—to the economy as much as to culture and politics, to what happens in markets as much as to what happens in communities and families.

Perhaps unexpectedly, the field of economics also offers resources for critiquing a reading of the plastics crisis as an exclusively (and intractably) economic problem. This may seem a surprising claim. It is certainly true that the discourse of mainstream economics regularly gives the sense that markets operate according to their own natural laws and thus often encourages the very compartmentalized worldview that CST so resoundingly rejects. Such rhetoric is indeed dangerous for our moral imaginations, given that it legitimates both a profits-only mindset within business and a kind of passive fatalism about what can be expected of

---

[5] See, e.g., Benedict XVI, *Caritas in Veritate* (June 29, 2009), www.vatican.va/content/benedict-xvi/en/encyclicals/documents/hf_ben-xvi_enc_20090629_caritas-in-veritate.html. See also Daniel Finn, ed., *The Moral Dynamics of Economic Life: An Extension and Critique of* Caritas in Veritate (Oxford University Press, 2012).

markets by those "outside" of them.⁶ However, underneath and despite this misleading rhetoric, economics also contains practical resources for thinking about how markets are deeply social institutions and how economic processes and outcomes are inevitably shaped by cultural, legal, and social factors. As a result, it offers useful tools for thinking outside the market-state binary that is so unhelpful for addressing complex social problems.⁷

Consider, for example, economic analyses of "social dilemmas" and "collective action problems," a category which includes the plastics crisis.⁸ These are situations in which individually-rational decisions lead to collective outcomes that are irrational and even devastating but where conflicting interests in the present discourage the very kind of cooperative action required to make all parties better off in the long term; the so-called "tragedy of the commons," where shared resources are overused until depleted, is one form these can take. The assumption that markets only work one way would lead to the conclusion that this tragedy is inevitable unless the state steps in, because rational market actors simply do not cooperate unless they are forced to.

As it turns out, however, empirical research in economics indicates that individuals and communities can and do cooperate all the time. This was one of the insights generated by Elinor Ostrom's Nobel prize-winning research on communities that successfully governed communal resources such as fisheries and forests *without* having these managed by a centralized state authority.⁹ Some of the insights arising from her work include: 1) that

---

⁶ For a more developed argument along these lines, see Christina McRorie, "Heterodox Economics, Social Ethics, and Inequality: New Tools for Thinking Critically About Markets and Economic Injustices," *Journal of Religious Ethics* 47, no. 2 (2019): 232–258.

⁷ On the shortcomings of a market versus state mentality, see *Caritas in Veritate*, no. 39, and David Cloutier, *The Vice of Luxury: Economic Excess in a Consumer Age* (Georgetown University Press, 2015), 5–8.

⁸ For one introduction to these from the perspective of economics, see Roger Congleton, *Solving Social Dilemmas: Ethics, Politics, and Prosperity* (Oxford University Press, 2022).

⁹ See Elinor Ostrom, *Governing the Commons: The Evolution of Institutions for Collective Action* (Cambridge University Press, 1990).

governance is actually all around us, because our lives are shaped by norms arising from formal and informal institutions alike; 2) that in decentralized settings with many centers of power, collaboration, and negotiation over these norms are frequent; and 3) that norms arising from informal institutions *can* be quite effective at addressing complex problems and averting tragedy, if the right social conditions are in place. In her Nobel Prize address, Ostrom urged policy makers not to think that the only fix for social dilemmas is to have the state itself restrict self-interested behavior in markets but to also focus on "the development of institutions that bring out the best in humans," fostering the kinds of communities that can themselves engage in effective collective action.[10]

I highlight this comment not to cast doubt on the indispensability of state action with regard to large-scale economic injustices, but because this is a perspective that underscores the deeply *social* nature of what happens in markets. Indeed, this research suggests that markets are as much shaped by social institutions and cultural norms as they are by any abstract and unchanging form of "economic rationality." As a result, while government will be part of the solution to economic injustices, other forms of action can make effective contributions as well.

Who Is Called to Live Out the Preferential Option for the Poor, and How?

Taking this broader view of the kinds of social activity shaping market activity, we can now ask again: what can be done about the plastics crisis and by whom? For Christians who believe that the gospel applies to all of social life, this is also a question about how we are called to live out Christ's preferential option for the poor: how can and should we love those who are most vulnerable to the harms of our current and increasing reliance on plastic?

---

[10] Elinor Ostrom, "Beyond Markets and States: Polycentric Governance of Complex Economic Systems," *American Economic Review* 100, no. 3 (2010): 664–665.

The remainder of this chapter considers this question from the perspective of different levels of society, beginning with government, moving to NGOs, businesses, and other organizations, and ending with families and individuals. With the resources of both CST and economics in mind, the goal in what follows will be briefly to ask how each of these are venues in which collective agency is exercised to shape what happens within markets—even if usually indirectly and sometimes with ambiguous effects—and thus, how these are also venues in which we are called to live out the option for the poor.

Government

While it would be a mistake to assume that government alone can effect real change in markets, this by no means undercuts its utter indispensability in protecting the common good. In the Catholic imagination, in fact, government is an important way that *"society as a whole"* acts together; which is to say, CST does not conceive of the state as an external power fundamentally opposed to social life or markets but as itself a medium of collective action.[11]

As a theologian, I will necessarily defer to policy experts on the exact form of the bans, taxes, subsidies, and other measures most appropriate for our current situation; the Minderoo-Monaco report contains a number of promising proposals. I will add that when we think about these proposals, it may be helpful to keep in mind Ostrom's advice to focus on building institutions that bring out "the best in us." How, we want to ask, can regulations make markets more hospitable to just and virtuous action—so that we are not just waiting for the state itself to enact a preferential option for the poor, but we are building an economy in which market actors themselves can live this out, too?

---

[11] US Conference of Catholic Bishops, *Economic Justice for All: Pastoral Letter on Catholic Social Teaching and the US Economy* (National Conference of Catholic Bishops, 1986), "A Pastoral Message: Economic Justice for All," no. 18. Italic in original.

Consider, for example, another finding emerging from empirical research in economics, indicating that markets are more likely to host behavior that is honest, fair, and even generous when they are characterized by transparency and competition.[12] Transparency (about industry practices or about the chemical contents of a product, for example) gives workers, vulnerable populations, and consumers the information required to make good choices, and competition gives them the options necessary to act on that information in ways that incentivize firms to respond accordingly. Where consumers have a moral preference (such as reducing plastics pollution or avoiding forever chemicals) and when they have real options among producers and access to reliable information about the products and practices of those producers, they can act on their values. Where information is not available, or consumers and others do not have real options, however, power is left unaccountably concentrated in the hands of firms.

Governments play an indispensable role in protecting healthy market competition and mandating appropriate forms of transparency and thus in ensuring an even distribution of economic agency. In a sense, measures implementing competition and transparency unlock the potential of market actors to improve markets from within, by acting on their preexisting values. Moreover, transparency itself can work to shift broader sensibilities and norms, as things like required labels can gently "nudge" us toward better decisions and render certain moral issues more socially salient.[13]

---

[12] See Christina G. McRorie, *The World of Markets* (Georgetown University Press, 2025).

[13] One dramatic illustration of this in action was the improvement in health standards after restaurants were required to visibly post hygiene grade cards. See Ginger Zhe Jin and Phillip Leslie, "The Effect of Information on Product Quality: Evidence from Restaurant Hygiene Grade Cards," *The Quarterly Journal of Economics* 118, no. 2 (2003): 409–451. For an accessible introduction to the broader conversation on nudging and its impact on social outcomes, see Richard Thaler and Cass Sunstein, *Nudge: The Final Edition* (Penguin Books, 2021).

Alongside regulation, we might also think about the state's role in shaping culture and technological progress, through public investments, such as endowments for the arts and humanities, and investments in medical and scientific research. How can these be oriented so that they help us envision a future that is different? And how can they be used to empower the voices and agency of the poor and marginalized, so that this envisioning process is collaborative and inclusive?

Non-Governmental Organizations

Similar questions can be asked of non-governmental organizations (NGOs), which have been growing in influence on the international business landscape in recent decades, in part as a way to respond to the failures of existing regulatory and enforcement structures to address economic injustices.[14] NGOs shape markets in a variety of ways, sometimes serving as "watchdogs" that increase transparency by reporting violations of existing standards and at other times pushing for changes to existing regulations and accepted corporate conduct. In this latter role, NGOs implement what some scholars have described as "private politics," both through political organizing and public advertising campaigns aimed to shift consumer perceptions of corporate practices or a specific firm's reputation.[15] Many of these efforts have been successful at changing individual firms' behaviors, and in some cases have even changed the practices of entire industries.[16] In a sense, NGOs thus already play an important role in effecting the option for the poor on a global scale.

---

[14] Michael Yaziji and Jonathan Doh, *NGOs and Corporations: Conflict and Collaboration* (Cambridge University Press, 2009).

[15] E.g., David Baron, "Private Politics," *Journal of Economics and Management Strategy* 12, no. 1 (2003): 31–66.

[16] E.g., see Gani Aldashev, Michela Limardi, and Thierry Verdier, "Watchdogs of the Invisible Hand: NGO Monitoring and Industry Equilibrium," *Journal of Development Economics* 116 (2016): 28–42.

In light of this impact, we can also ask: How are different NGOs currently addressing the plastics crisis, and what additional roles could and should they play? How are NGOs positioned to improve corporate practices, influence legislation, shift public discourse, and develop and foster creative local responses to pollution and plastics-related health problems? And how can governments, businesses, and other agencies support this work, either financially or in other ways? As individuals, for example, can we give key organizations a wider platform for their message, whether on social media or in our classrooms, in our churches or at our places of work? Given their support for smaller non-profits around the world, supporting international NGOs would seem to offer one concrete way for those in developed nations to try to empower grassroots efforts in developing contexts and thus include the marginalized in the process of collaborative problem-solving, even if indirectly and from a distance.[17]

Businesses and Other Organizations that Make Economic Decisions

Business firms are in a similar position to influence what goes on in global markets, and accordingly they have their own responsibility to enact the preferential option for the poor. Indeed, CST views business as a specific vocation to serve the common good and invites business leaders to reflect on the distinct opportunities they encounter to serve and be "*in solidarity with the poor.*"[18] How, we can ask, could and should the employees and leaders of firms in different industries—from finance to cosmetics to food production—creatively serve the poor by helping us envision an economy

---

[17] For brevity's sake this assumes an unambiguously supportive relationship between international NGOs and local agency; a fuller analysis of the role that NGOs play in implementing the preferential option would need to also address the recurrence of paternalistic and colonialist dynamics in development and humanitarian aid.

[18] Dicastery for Promoting Integral Human Development, *Vocation of the Business Leader: A Reflection*, 5th edition (2018), no. 45, www.humandevelopment.va/en/risorse/documenti/vocation-of-the-business-leader-a-reflection-5th-edition.html. Italics in original.

less dependent on plastics, and in so doing also work to reshape the accepted norms of their industries?[19]

It should be added that for-profit enterprises are not the only organizations that exercise economic agency and influence the economy. Social enterprises, non-profits, cooperatives, and universities all hire employees and contractors, construct and lease buildings, invest savings, purchase inputs and materials, offer products and services for sale, design advertising that has implicit values, and so forth—as do churches, libraries, hospitals, and even homeowners' associations and academic societies. In the Christian imagination, then, these are each also venues in which we are called to make a fundamental commitment to prioritizing the needs of the marginalized, and to addressing systemic injustices.

On the surface, this commitment will necessarily mean asking about the physical use of plastics in these communities. That said, it will also be critical to reflect on how these are settings in which we negotiate and collaborate on social norms and visions of the good life, too—or, put differently, on how these venues each host a kind of collective cultural governance. What do libraries, hospitals, and universities put on our radar as important to care about, through their programming and websites and campuses, and what habits do they model and facilitate? How do they each make a bid to shape what their employees, patrons, students, customers, and the wider public notice, and what they care about—and who has influence over how they do this?

For example, can medical schools train pediatricians to teach new parents about the health dangers of certain plastics, or can universities solicit donations for research centers aimed at understanding and addressing the health impacts of plastic? What about business schools? Business schools exercise a tremendous influence on the values, sensibilities, and moral imaginations that their students bring into the

---

[19] For more on the capacities and responsibilities of businesses to influence the industries in which they operate, see Martin Schlag, "Are Businesses Responsible for the Moral Ecology in Which They Operate?" in *Business Ethics and Catholic Social Thought*, ed. Daniel K. Finn (Georgetown University Press, 2021), 163–179.

workforce. As a result, those who work and teach at or donate to business schools have a special responsibility to use their positions to promote ethical entrepreneurship. How can business school curricula and programming encourage forms of enterprise that creatively resist a mindlessly plasticized future, include the poor in global markets, and encourage cultures of solidarity?

Families and Individuals

Finally, what are the capacities and thus responsibilities of families and individuals? While it is important not to let a focus on individual agency eclipse larger institutional concerns, a good deal of academic and pastoral scholarship has quite rightly critiqued the wasteful nature of the contemporary American lifestyle, and calls to reduce plastics consumption often feature in exhortations to eco-discipleship.[20] Instead of repeating that (very good) advice, I want to highlight our role in shaping culture more broadly and in indirectly but collectively contributing to the governance of markets. We know we have a responsibility to prudently exercise our political right to vote, and we are generally aware that we are also "voting" for the economy to be a certain way every time we spend money. However, in addition to our roles as citizens and consumers, we also contribute to collective governance in other ways, even if these are inevitably indirect and diffuse.

How we do this will vary from person to person, since we each participate in different communities and exercise different forms of power within those communities. But in these communities, too, many of the above questions will apply: where do we work, live, shop, worship, and recreate, and do we have any influence over the decisions that these communities make and over the values and sensibilities they foster in others? Can we encourage our children's schools to reduce their reliance

---

[20] On the danger of the "individualization of responsibility," for example, see Michael Maniates, "Individualization: Plant a Tree, Buy a Bike, Save the World?," *Global Environmental Politics* 1, no. 3 (August 2001): 31–52.

on single-use plastics and to include the plastics crisis in their science curriculum? Do we have any influence over what happens in the breakrooms and cafeterias at our places of work?

In our relationships more generally, how do we speak about our consumption choices and the purpose of business? Do we fall prey to dualistic thinking that fatalistically separates moral concerns from economic ones? For example, are we inadvertently teaching our children that success in life requires a good income and that *after* they secure this, *then* they can do good by making charitable donations? Or—just as unhelpfully—do we cynically refer to careers in finance and industry as intrinsically materialistic and for "sellouts," as if business itself could not contribute to the common good? Or, do we view the economy in an integrated way, and encourage others to do so, too?

Conclusion

Although the disproportionate harms visited upon the most vulnerable call for drastic change to our current trajectory of producing, using, and disposing of ever-more plastics, the very scale of the crisis can make it seem that this change can only come from authorities at "the top." When considering the global economic factors driving this trajectory, it is tempting to conclude that the "rest of us" are effectively powerless until governments step in to stop markets from doing what they do "naturally." This chapter opened by admitting a great deal of truth to this picture, above all with regard to the necessity of coordinated political action to set limits on the production and disposal of plastics. Even so, it has argued that both economics and CST offer resources for viewing the economy—and thus the plastics crisis—in somewhat less two-dimensional terms.

Instead, this chapter has argued for a perspective that takes into account the deeply social nature of all economic activity and thus the way that market processes and outcomes are sustained and shaped by a range of cultural norms and practices. Such a view broadens our sense of who participates in economic governance and of what forms of action can be taken to steer global and local economies away from our mindlessly increasing reliance on plastics. For those who believe that the most vulnerable deserve to be most prioritized in collective decision-making, this opens up important questions about how to use whatever agency we have, in whatever roles we occupy, to work toward a healthier and more just world.

Christina G. McRorie, PhD, is associate professor of moral theology at the Gloria L. and Charles I. Clough School of Theology and Ministry at Boston College. Her research is interdisciplinary and draws from the Christian tradition, political economy, and economics to consider questions about moral agency and obligation in markets. She currently serves on the board of directors of the Society of Christian Ethics, and on the editorial boards of the *Journal of Moral Theology* and the *Journal of Catholic Social Thought*. From 2020 to 2023 she was a Research Fellow in the Collaborative Inquiries in Christian Theological Anthropology project funded through the John Templeton Foundation. Before joining Boston College she taught at Creighton University for seven years. She also has experience leading low-income financial empowerment programming, including two years coordinating volunteer tax preparation sites with the Boston Earned Income Tax Credit (EITC) Coalition. She published *The World of Markets* (Georgetown University Press, 2025), a monograph that uses the theological category of "the world" to examine markets as contexts for moral agency.

7. The Plastics Crisis and Catholic Social Teaching

Andrea Vicini, SJ

A global crisis so expansive and pervasive as the ongoing plastic crisis challenges humankind and the planet on many accounts. Global awareness is urgently needed. In the preceding chapters, scientists raise concerns. As ethicists, we trust their expertise, and we examine it critically. We heard the urgent cry of scientists, calling for a strong commitment to address this planetary crisis, to care for the health and wellbeing of human beings, and to protect the planet for our generation and for future generations. We join them arguing for concrete solutions.

Hence, the beginning of the needed ethical response to the global crisis caused by plastic production, disposal, accumulation, and pollution is centered on *trust*. Together with Catholic social thought, ethicists *trust* scientists, healthcare professionals, politicians, activists, believers, and educators who critically examine the productive cycle of plastics as well as its uses and who struggle to find solutions.[1] The social and environmental responses, which address how much humankind relies on and depends on plastic, discarding it, being unable to recycle it effectively, and accumulating it in our oceans and landfills, build on this *trust*. Ethically, we neither question nor doubt the urgency of the plastic crisis.

However, trust calls on trust and depends on trust. Collectively, we need to trust our commitment and our ability to respond ethically to this crisis. As a society, and as people of good will, Catholic social thought empowers us to respond to the global plastic crisis in ways that depend on this trust and strive to strengthen our ability to be trustworthy in caring for humankind and for our planet.

---

[1] See James F. Keenan, "Social Trust and the Ethics of Our Institutions," *Journal of the Society of Christian Ethics* 42, no. 2 (2022): 245–263.

An appropriate ethical response should identify necessary approaches and concrete steps as part of a comprehensive *ethical strategy*. This response should recognize and appreciate practical solutions and initiatives that are already implemented, mostly locally. In what follows I highlight key elements that characterize this ethical strategy and qualify an ethical approach informed by Catholic social thought. I focus, first, on what concerns *personal and social* engagements; second, on *political and economic* dimensions; third, on *technological and critical* approaches.

1. Personal and Social

What should we do to address the ethical challenges of plastic pollution both on a local and global scale? Usually, the first response focuses on the *individual* and on one's responsibilities articulated in terms of *duties*, for example, to consume less plastic and to recycle. This emphasis on personal duties indicates that one's moral life is understood mostly as a set of norms that need to be fulfilled at the individual level. By fulfilling these norms, one acts rightly and avoids the sense of guilt that might be experienced in being unable to tackle the complexity of the global plastic crisis. Individual duties that can be fulfilled seem to protect a person from feeling overwhelmed by the extent of the plastic crisis. Moreover, one can experience self-gratification and affirm to have been able to do something, what duty called one to do.

However, we are aware that the impact of individual choices is quantitatively irrelevant compared to the extent of plastic pollution, as well as when one considers the dynamics and interests that inform plastic production, distribution, and use. What can an individual realistically do? As individuals, is there any possible way to have a larger and more significant impact in addressing the ongoing and increasing plastic pollution? Answering in the negative seems to be the only option. But dismissing what individuals can do might lead to disillusionment, disappointment, hopelessness, maybe even despair, by assuming that nothing that really matters can be done.

An ethical approach centered on the individual and on one's duties is needed, but it is insufficient. Both an individualistic focus and a deontological ethics show their limitations. An ethical approach that expands its attention to diversified moral agents—that is, by considering that individuals belong to communities, networks,[2] collectives,[3] and institutions—seems to be more promising. Such an expanded ethical approach is more capacious and accounts for the interconnectedness and interdependence that characterize moral agents. Hence, "Everything is interconnected," as Pope Francis stressed in his 2015 encyclical letter *Laudato Si': On Care for Our Common Home*.[4] We are not isolated, unencumbered beings. Moreover, just behavior could be fostered neither merely nor exclusively by a sense of duty but, more successfully, by the attraction of what is just, right, and good. Virtues seem to be more appropriate to describe how moral agents, in their multiplicity and difference, can embrace virtuous behaviors—even when facing the daunting plastic crisis. Through habituation the moral agents live virtuous lives. Moreover, virtuous moral agents contribute to a virtuous society.

---

[2] For David Hollenbach, "Governance from above by sovereign governments must today be complemented by networks linking groups across borders in complex webs of mutual dependence. People who are networked together can begin to recognize that their own interests and the interests of others in the network are intertwined. They begin to pursue goals other than maximization of self-interest.... Through networking, different groups can work together in a participatory way—in collaboration without domination, in mutual support without hegemony.... Governance through collaborative, participatory networking holds real promise as a way to advance the transnational common good.... the promotion of local, regional and global cooperation for the common good through polycentric governance and networking.... Collaboration in networks requires a degree of trust among those who participate." David Hollenbach, SJ, "The Glory of God and the Global Common Good: Solidarity in a Turbulent Word," *Proceedings of the Catholic Theological Society of America* 72 (2017): 55.

[3] See James F. Keenan, "Recognizing Collectives as Moral Agents," *Theological Studies* 85, no. 1 (2024): 96–123.

[4] Francis, *Laudato Si': On Care for Our Common Home* (2015), www.vatican.va/content/francesco/en/encyclicals/documents/papa-francesco_20150524_enciclica-laudato-si.html, no. 70.

Among the many personal and social virtues that can be highlighted, *prudence* and *justice* could be mentioned. Individual and collective choices are informed by a prudential approach that aims at considering benefits and advantages, as well as costs and consequences—for individuals, communities, and the whole planet. Moreover, longing for justice leads to promoting social justice by highlighting ongoing injustices and inequities and striving to promote greater just dynamics and equity.

Hence, prudence and justice could accompany citizens in their personal and social striving to act in virtuous ways in a virtuous society. As outcomes, more prudential choices would lead, for example, to limit plastic production, to promote incentives, to seek alternative solutions, to demand accountability, and to require commitments to clean up.

A virtuous approach presupposes *togetherness* and aims at fostering *solidarity*.[5] As citizens, we are experiencing the consequences of plastic polluting the water that we drink,[6] the food that we grow and eat, and the air that we breathe. Together we strive for a world less polluted by plastic. We join others who preceded us in their commitments to find alternative ways of living, producing, consuming, and discarding. We commit ourselves to work together, in solidarity with those who are already experiencing in their bodies, homes, and working places the consequences

---

[5] See Meghan J. Clark, *The Vision of Catholic Social Thought: The Virtue of Solidarity and the Praxis of Human Rights* (Fortress Press, 2014); Meghan J. Clark, "Health Equity, Solidarity and the Common Good: Who Lives, Who Dies, Who Tells Your Story," *Health Progress* 97, no. 6 (2016): 9–12; Meghan J. Clark, "Pope Francis and the Christological Dimensions of Solidarity in Catholic Social Teaching," *Theological Studies* 80, no. 1 (2019): 102–122; Meghan. J. Clark, "Anatomy of a Social Virtue: Solidarity and Corresponding Vices," *Political Theology* 15, no. 1 (2014): 26–39.

[6] On clean water, see Susan K. Barnett, "Water, Sanitation and Hygiene: Vatican, Catholic Health Care Take Leadership Roles in 'Wash' Work," *Health Progress* 102, no. 4 (2021): 38–44; Christiana Z. Peppard, *Just Water: Theology, Ethics, and Fresh Water Crises*, revised ed., Ecology and Justice (Orbis Books, 2018); Vatican Dicastery for Promoting Integral Human Development, "Aqua Fons Vitae: Orientations on Water, Symbol of the Cry of the Poor and the Cry of the Earth" (2020), www.humandevelopment.va/en/risorse/documenti/aqua-fons-vitae-the-new-document-of-the-dicastery-now-available.html.

of plastic pollution, aiming at reducing and, if possible, eliminating what can affect the health of people and of the planet.

One example is needed. In March 2024 the prestigious *New England Journal of Medicine* published the results of a study aimed at verifying the assumption that, as the authors indicate, "Microplastics and nanoplastics (MNPs) are emerging as a potential risk factor for cardiovascular disease in preclinical studies."[7] In particular, they wrote that

> Several studies have shown that microplastics and nanoplastics (MNPs) enter the human body through ingestion, inhalation, and skin exposure, where they interact with tissues and organs. MNPs have been found in selected human tissues, such as the placenta, lungs, and liver, as well as in breast milk, urine, and blood. Recent studies performed in preclinical models have led to the suggestion of MNPs as a new risk factor for cardiovascular diseases.[8]

To verify this suggestion, "A total of 304 patients were enrolled in the study.... Polyethylene was detected in carotid artery plaque of 150 patients (58.4%)."[9] Moreover, the authors continue, "In this study, patients with carotid artery plaque in which MNPs were detected had a higher risk of a composite of myocardial infarction, stroke, or death from any cause at thirty-four months of follow-up than those in whom MNPs were not detected."[10] It is sobering to discover that one can find MNPs everywhere, including within human bodies, inside artery plaques.

---

[7] Raffaele Marfella, Francesco Prattichizzo, Celestino Sardu, Gianluca Fulgenzi, Laura Graciotti, Tatiana Spadoni, et al., "Microplastics and Nanoplastics in Atheromas and Cardiovascular Events," *New England Journal of Medicine* 390, no. 10 (2024): 900.

[8] Marfella, et al., "Microplastics and Nanoplastics in Atheromas and Cardiovascular Events," 901.

[9] Marfella, et al., "Microplastics and Nanoplastics in Atheromas and Cardiovascular Events," 900.

[10] Marfella, et al., "Microplastics and Nanoplastics in Atheromas and Cardiovascular Events," 900.

Caution is needed when one focuses on statistical risk, as the moral theologian Paul Scherz strongly stresses in his volume recently published on *The Ethics of Precision Medicine*.[11] As moral agents and as a society striving to be virtuous, ethical choices in healthcare are not solely determined by calculating percentages of risk, with a false understanding of what predictive medicine could offer to society. When one considers the relationship between patients and healthcare professionals in healthcare settings, or when one looks at the health of populations and their living environments, or focuses on global health, ethical decision-making aimed at promoting health requires a careful *discernment* of the many factors that intervene in influencing health and its pursuit, particularly when one considers how human and planetary health are threatened by plastic pollution.

The virtue of solidarity helps to address this demanding discernment because, as Pope John Paul II stressed, solidarity "is not a feeling of vague compassion or shallow distress at the misfortunes of so many people, both near and far. On the contrary, it is a firm and persevering determination to commit oneself to the common good; that is to say to the good of all and of each individual, because we are all really responsible for all."[12]

Catholic social thought embodies this vision of the person interconnected, interdependent, in solidarity with others, striving to join those who are less well off, in greater need, marginalized, and excluded, working together with them to foster social ways of living that are more virtuous, and that contribute to promote what is good in inclusive ways, for individuals, societies, and the whole planet. When one considers the environment and health, this comprehensive ethical approach aims to promote agency and empowerment, by assuming that personal and

---

[11] Paul Joseph Scherz, *The Ethics of Precision Medicine: The Problems of Prevention in Healthcare* (University of Notre Dame Press, 2024).

[12] John Paul II, "*Sollicitudo Rei Socialis*: For the Twentieth Anniversary of *Populorum Progressio*" (1987), http://www.vatican.va/content/john-paul-ii/en/encyclicals/documents/hf_jp-ii_enc_30121987_sollicitudo-rei-socialis.html, no. 38.

collective agency and empowerment can help civil society to address the urgent challenges raised by plastic pollution.

2. Political and Economic

To promote the common good, Catholic social thought focuses both on individuals and society. This double emphasis implies that needed attention is given to political choices and economic strategies as well as structures and systems. For example, the industrial complex is the result of multiple structures and could be considered a system that, across continents, is responsible for the production of plastic in ways that should be the object of critical scrutiny. Is the industrial system more attentive to its self-preservation and expansion than to ways of producing, distributing, and then discarding that should be challenged by society as a whole? Should the industrial compact build-in, together with the cost of plastic production, also the cost of preventing plastics from ending up in our bodies, in our food, on our beaches—mostly in countries in the Global South of the world—and become a troubling burden of our collective inheritance, which we leave to the current generation and to those who will follow us?

When one considers structures, political and economic forces contribute to articulating social dynamics in terms of power. As citizens, we stress the responsibilities that we assign to structures, with their dynamics and social institutions, to serve the common good in ways that foster social justice and make a preferential option for the poor, while caring for our planet.

3. Technological and Critical

Within the social context, whether in the fields of scientific research or in the industrial complex, technology demands a particular ethical attention.

For many, technology is the exclusive and unique answer to the challenges that humankind faces, including plastic pollution.

In more nuanced ways, ethically we stress that while we ask technology to provide and make available technological developments that can contain and limit the production, use, accumulation, and disposal of plastics, we are aware that exclusive technological answers are incomplete. To presume that technology is *the* only solution and that technological fixes alone can respond to what affects human beings and the planet betrays what Pope Francis has called the "technocratic paradigm."[13] We assume that the ethical and social problems that technology has created can only be addressed and solved by more technology, and in ways which we presume we are able to control. In doing so we lack a critical assessment of technology and of its achievements, failures, and applications. We implement an extractive approach, "attempting to extract everything possible"[14] from who and what surround us. We also miss learning from the history of science and, in particular, of technology, where we can trace reductionist and deterministic approaches, informed by biased vision of the self, society, race, gender, and development. We also perpetuate the extractivism that has shaped the global colonial history and continue to inform neocolonial dynamics across continents.

If we assume that technology has all the answers to social challenges, we avoid situating technology within the social, political, historical, and economic contexts in which technology has developed and continues to grow. As in the case of science, technology is not neutral. Hence, personal, communal, and social trust in technological solutions should be informed by a critical hermeneutic able to unmask how technological developments might demand more and more technology to deal with some of the consequences that the technology caused in the first place. The technological production of plastics demands more technologies able to

---

[13] Francis, *Laudato Si'*, nos. 106–109.
[14] Francis, *Laudato Si'*, no. 106.

contain the negative effects of plastics. We should strive for ways to slow down, contain, and break this entrapping technological spiral.

Moreover, the technocratic paradigm allows us to recognize ways in which technologies manifest *social control*. Within society, we presume our ability to control the technologies that we developed, but these technologies also control us by imposing themselves on us.

Of course, technologies do not have moral agency. They express the control of specific moral agents, who promote their use and, in doing so, increase our dependence. We are aware of how much we depend on plastics, in all sectors of social life. By examining our dependence, we can identify and name specific moral agents and the structures that they foster, for example, in the case of national and multinational companies producing plastics. But there are ways in which the individual and collective moral agency is constrained, controlled, and limited, for example, when we think of social pressures to depend on plastics and its convenience. Hence, the technocratic paradigm invites us to articulate a critical assessment of technological developments and to strengthen our social awareness and critical engagements, which might imply promoting environmentally sustainable alternatives and embracing forms of resistance to unquestioned uses of plastic products.

Conclusion

Catholic social thought focuses on moral agents and on their agency, fostering their commitment to promote the common good, as well as on structures and institutions. To have a concrete impact, and address the challenges of plastic pollution, at the local level the actions and initiatives of grassroots organizations, towns, and neighborhoods are essential. Globally, networks play important roles by expanding moral agency. This commitment to social justice relies on pragmatic solutions embraced by individuals, collectives, and institutions. At the same time, even focused initiatives—like the ban of plastic bags or using cutlery and single-serving food containers that are compostable—are part of needed more challenging structural transformations and modified productive engagements on a national and global scale. Moreover, international agreements, treaties, and regulations aim at promoting national and global commitments. Finally, education and formation are integral to the ongoing task of empowering moral agents and fostering needed structural transformations and changes. Catholic social thought joins these efforts that express human ingenuity and strive to promote better living conditions for humankind and the planet.

Andrea Vicini, SJ, is the Chair of the Theology Department and Michael P. Walsh Professor of Bioethics, and an affiliate member of the Gloria L. and Charles I. Clough School of Theology and Ministry at Boston College. A pediatrician (MD, University of Bologna), he is an alumnus of Boston College (STL and PhD) and holds an STD from the Pontifical Faculty of Theology of Southern Italy (Naples). He held the Boston College Gasson Chair and has taught in Italy, Albania, Mexico, Chad, and France. He is co-chair of the international network Catholic Theological Ethics in the World Church. His research and publications include theological bioethics, sustainability, global public health, new biotechnologies, and fundamental theological ethics. During the academic year 2015–2016, he had a research fellowship at the Center of Theological Inquiry in Princeton, NJ, on the Societal Implications of Astrobiology. Since 2021 he has been a Fellow of the Collegium Ramazzini.

Part 4

Striving *for* Solutions

8. Advancing a Global Treaty on Plastic Pollution: Current Status and Challenge

Margaret Spring and Cindy Matuch

Since synthetic plastic was first developed in the early twentieth century, use and production has grown exponentially. In 1950, the world produced just two million metric tons of plastic per year.[1] By 2019, annual global use reached 460 million metric tons, and that amount is expected to nearly triple by 2060.[2] Every year, it is estimated that nineteen to twenty-three million metric tons of this plastic leaks into the aquatic environment alone—polluting lakes, rivers, and oceans.[3] Today, the petroleum and chemical composition of many plastics, as well as plastic waste, is causing detrimental impacts to the climate, the environment, wildlife and ecosystems, and human health.[4] In short, along with use and production, plastic pollution and its negative impacts have grown exponentially. Whole and broken-down plastics are readily seen on our streets and in our waterways, but they have also permeated the deepest parts of our oceans, the air above our tallest mountains, the food we eat, the water we drink, and our own bodies.

Basis for Negotiations: UNEA Resolution 5/14

---

[1] See Hannah Ritchie, Veronika Samborska, and Max Roser, "Plastic Pollution," *Our World in Data* (2023), ourworldindata.org/plastic-pollution.

[2] See Philip J. Landrigan, Hervé Raps, Maureen Cropper, Caroline Bald, Manuel Brunner, Elvia Maya Canonizado, et al., "The Minderoo-Monaco Commission on Plastics and Human Health," *Annals of Global Health* 89, no. 1 (2023): 1–215.

[3] See United Nations Environment Programme, "Plastic Pollution," www.unep.org/plastic-pollution.

[4] See Martin Wagner, Laura Monclús, Hans Peter H. Arp, Ksenia J. Groh, Mari E. Løseth, Jane Muncke, et al., "State of the Science on Plastic Chemicals: Identifying and Addressing Chemicals and Polymers of Concern" (2024), doi.org/10.5281/zenodo.10701706.

The global effort to establish a treaty addressing plastic pollution has been a complex, multi-year process involving numerous stakeholders and a series of critical negotiations. This initiative was formally launched in March 2022, when during the resumed 5th session of the United Nations Environment Assembly (UNEA) (known as UNEA 5.2) over 175 countries approved UNEA Resolution 5/14, which called for the development of an international legally-binding agreement to tackle plastic pollution, including in the marine environment. The specific mandate was to develop an instrument, based on a comprehensive approach that addresses the full life cycle of plastic, and that would include both binding and voluntary approaches.

Specifically, the Resolution called for specific elements to be included in the instrument, such as:

- Objectives for the instrument
- Promoting sustainable production and consumption
- Promoting cooperative measures to reduce plastic pollution
- National action plans toward preventing, reducing and eliminating plastic pollution
- National reporting
- Periodic assessment of implementation progress
- Assessment of effectiveness toward achieving objectives
- Increasing knowledge
- Encouraging action across sectors (including a "multi-stakeholder action agenda")
- Capacity building and technical assistance
- Promoting research and development
- Addressing compliance

It also asked the Intergovernmental Negotiating Committee (INC) to consider:

- Obligations, measures and voluntary approaches
- Need for a financial mechanism to support the implementation
- Flexibility, taking into account national circumstances
- The best available science, traditional knowledge, knowledge of indigenous peoples, and local knowledge systems
- Lessons learned and best practices
- The possibility of a mechanism to provide policy-relevant scientific and socioeconomic information and assessment related to plastic pollution; and
- Efficient organization and streamlined secretariat arrangements

That same year, the United Nations Environment Programme (UNEP) established the Intergovernmental Negotiating Committee (INC) to advance the work in accordance with Resolution 5/14, "with the ambition of completing its work by 2024," and the ultimate goal of adopting a comprehensive legally-binding agreement by 2025.[5]

Progress on Negotiations 2022–2024

Negotiations officially began in 2022 with the first INC meeting in Uruguay (INC-1), which set the foundational elements for what would later become the "Zero Draft" of the treaty.[6] Working documents provided and compiled by the Secretariat included potential "options" and

---

[5] United Nations Environment Assembly (UNEA), "Resolution 5/14: End Plastic Pollution: Towards an International Legally-Binding Instrument," Resolution Adopted by the United Nations Environmental Assembly (2022), digitallibrary.un.org/record/3999257.
[6] United Nations Environment Programme (UNEP), *Report of the Intergovernmental Negotiating Committee to Develop an Internationally Legally-Binding Instrument on Plastic Pollution, Including in the Marine Environment, First Session* (United Nations Environment Programme, 2022).

"elements" for such a draft, as well as a "glossary of key terms" and a "plastic science" document.[7]

Subsequent meetings in France, Kenya, and Canada continued consideration of the key elements that would form part of a treaty text, gradually moving the process forward. In France, the Chair of the meeting was tasked with preparing a "Zero Draft" text of the international legally-binding instrument. The draft incorporated views expressed during the committee's first and second session, as well as proposals submitted during the intersessional period.[8] The scientific community emphasized the need for robust, multidisciplinary evidence to guide the treaty's development, including addressing plastics' full lifecycle and their widespread environmental and health impacts.

The third negotiating meeting in Kenya marked the beginning of textual negotiations. The scientific community urged action to be guided by integrated, interdisciplinary research to address the plastic pollution crisis comprehensively, emphasizing the need for solutions that respect cultural diversity and address socioeconomic vulnerabilities. However, member states' review of the "Zero Draft" revealed divergent opinions on key treaty elements, such as plastic production and chemicals of concern.

---

[7] United Nations Environment Programme, *Broad Options for the Structure of the International Legally-Binding Instrument on Plastic Pollution, Including in the Marine Environment, Taking into Account Paragraphs 3 and 4 of United Nations Environment Assembly Resolution 5/14* (Punta del Este, Uruguay, 2022); United Nations Environment Programme, *Potential Elements, Based on Provisions in Paragraphs 3 and 4 of United Nations Environment Assembly Resolution 5/14, Including Key Concepts, Procedures and Mechanisms of Legally-Binding Multilateral Agreements that May Be Relevant to Furthering Implementation and Compliance Under the Future International Legally-Binding Instrument on Plastic Pollution, Including in the Marine Environment* (Punta del Este, Uruguay, 2022); United Nations Environment Programme, *Glossary of Key Terms* (Punta del Este, Uruguay, 2022); United Nations Environment Programme, *Plastic Science* (Punta del Este, Uruguay, 2022).

[8] United Nations Environmental Programme, *Report of the Intergovernmental Negotiating Committee to Develop an Internationally Legally-Binding Instrument on Plastic Pollution, Including in the Marine Environment, on the Work of its Second Session* (Paris, 2023).

These disagreements resulted in the draft becoming heavily bracketed, culminating in a seventy-page document later referred to as the "Revised Zero Draft." Despite the need for further revisions, member states failed to agree on intersessional work to refine the draft ahead of the fourth meeting, leaving no formal mandate for such work. Consequently, informal efforts emerged to develop interim products, such as Switzerland drafting proposals addressing chemicals of concern and problematic or avoidable plastic products.

At the fourth negotiation meeting in Canada, discussions focused on the heavily-bracketed "Revised Zero Draft" compiled after the Kenya meeting. Some areas of greater convergence emerged, including around addressing plastic waste management and ensuring a just transition. The scientific community highlighted the critical need for a treaty to address the human health risks and adopt precautionary measures informed by scientific and Indigenous advice. However, significant divergence persisted regarding provisions on plastic production, chemicals and polymers of concern, and the overall scope of the instrument. For the first time, delegates agreed on formal intersessional work, with outputs to be considered at the fifth negotiating meeting in the Republic of Korea. Two ad hoc intersessional open-ended expert groups were established: 1) an expert group to develop potential sources and means for the establishment of a financial mechanism, and 2) an expert group to analyze criteria and non-criteria-based approaches with regard to plastic products and chemicals of concern in plastic products and product design, primarily focusing on recyclability and reusability. Additionally, a legal-drafting group was established to begin its work at the fifth session.[9]

The fifth meeting of the INC (INC-5) was held in Busan, Republic of Korea, from November 25 to December 1, 2024, and was intended to be the final round of negotiations. However, while it brought several

---

[9] United Nations Environment Programme, *Report of the Intergovernmental Negotiating Committee to Develop an Internationally Legally-Binding Instrument on Plastic Pollution, Including in the Marine Environment, on the Work of its Fourth Session* (UNEP, 2024).

advancements, the meeting ultimately concluded without agreement on a final treaty text. Delegates agreed to reconvene in 2025 for a subsequent session, INC-5.2, to continue deliberations on a "Chair's Text" that was circulated to INC members on December 1, 2024.[10]

Despite the lack of resolution, INC-5 saw both significant progress and persistent challenges, signaling cautious optimism about the treaty's future. One of the notable achievements of INC-5 was the increased ambition displayed by a growing number of member states. Over one hundred countries expressed support for the text's proposals to reduce the production of primary plastic polymers in alignment with global targets, emphasizing the urgency of addressing the upstream drivers of plastic pollution. Additionally, ninety-four countries backed a declaration calling for legally-binding obligations to phase out the most harmful plastic products and chemicals of concern. Eighty-five members supported a declaration referencing four key measures that would form part of an ambitious instrument. These declarations demonstrated a rising commitment to ambitious action, though they also underscored the deep divides that persist within the INC.

The "Chair's Text," which will serve as the basis for the next session, reflects the Chair's perspective on the current state of the negotiations. Many member states agreed on the importance of integrating human health considerations into the treaty text, with discussions slated to consider either strengthening references to health within the provisions or including a standalone health provision. A global target for reducing primary plastic polymer production to sustainable levels has been incorporated into the "Chair's Text" as a key option. There was also broad recognition of the need for predictable and equitable financing mechanisms, especially for developing countries, though specific modalities remain a point of contention. The Chair has noted that he saw

---

[10] Intergovernmental Negotiating Committee to Develop an International Legally-Binding Instrument on Plastic Pollution, Including in the Marine Environment, *Chair's Text* (Ottawa, 2024).

points of convergence, and he explained that there was divergence on issues that prevented the Committee from reaching consensus.

Fundamental disagreements remain over key aspects of the treaty, including its overall scope. The High Ambition Coalition of sixty-seven members has continued to promote addressing the full life cycle of plastics, encompassing production, consumption, and disposal. In contrast, members of the Like-Minded Countries (LMC) group, which includes major oil-producing states and large plastic producers, continue to prefer a more limited approach centered on downstream measures, such as waste management. The regulation of chemicals of concern in plastics has also emerged as a contentious issue. Some countries view these measures as essential to protecting human health and the environment, while others have labeled this a "redline" (meaning they are opposed to addressing the chemical composition of plastics within the treaty framework), citing that chemicals are addressed in other global regulatory frameworks and/or can be addressed nationally.

Financing for the treaty's implementation has proven similarly challenging to negotiate, with debates about who should contribute to financing the treaty's implementation, the balance between public and private sources of funding, and the form of the financial mechanism. Developing nations and coalitions such as the African Group and Pacific Small Island Developing States (PSIDS) have emphasized the need for predictable and equitable funding, particularly for developing countries. Several text proposals were introduced during INC-5. However, reaching agreement on the form and function of a financial mechanism for the treaty has been challenging, as member states continue to debate issues of responsibility and resource allocation.

The Road Ahead: 2025 and Beyond

Looking ahead, reaching convergence on several key areas will be needed to finalize a meaningful initial treaty text. The eighty-five members who supported the "Stand Up for Ambition" statement have clearly indicated what they consider essential elements of a text, but the content and detail of those elements remain to be elaborated, including in ways that could be supported by an even wider array of members.

The consideration of the health impacts of plastics and ways that health protection will be integrated in the treaty measures has gained increasing attention over the course of the negotiations, with a majority of member states in support of including the protection of human health as a core objective of the treaty. This aligns with the approach taken in many other multilateral environmental agreements and reflects the growing recognition of the interconnectedness between environmental and human health, as well as the need for science-based measures to mitigate risks. While there is widely held alignment on an objective of protection of human health, the essential elements of this protection also remain to be determined in the continuing discussions.

Health—and environmental—protection will also be supported by the establishment of a scientific advisory body to support the treaty's implementation. While there is broad agreement on the need for scientific input, the form, function, and composition of such a body have yet to be defined. There is an opportunity to consider appropriate models, based on experience from other instruments and analysis of their effectiveness, to inform the future discussions on the establishment, composition and terms of reference of such a body, including to ensure that the science and technical advice that will inform the treaty's implementation and its evolution is free of conflicts of interest. Establishing an effective science-policy interface and science advisory mechanism will help to inform effectiveness evaluation of the treaty and ensure that it remains adaptive and responsive to emerging scientific knowledge, thereby enhancing its effectiveness over time. Coupled with this, effective decision-making and adjustment mechanisms will be key—as highlighted by those nations that supported the "Stand Up for Ambition Statement." Negotiators have not yet tackled the question of decision thresholds head-on, but precedent supports determining an appropriate majority threshold for decisions where no consensus can be reached.[11]

The United States has played a key role in the negotiations through the end of 2024. The US is not a member of either the High Ambition Coalition or the Like-Minded Countries group and has sought to play a bridging role and find the proverbial "big tent" that all members could converge within. Ahead of INC-5, the US made its clearest statements of ambition to date, expressing support for reducing the production and consumption of primary plastic polymers and emphasizing the value of global criteria for addressing problematic plastic products and chemicals of concern. Nevertheless, the US did not join the group of over one hundred countries on a text proposal towards a global target and has not supported globally-binding obligations associated with such criteria, proposing instead—at INC-5—a menu of possible national actions which could be taken. Looking ahead, the change in US administration in 2025 is likely to further complicate the geopolitical landscape for environmental multilateralism and the conclusion of the plastics treaty negotiations.

As negotiations move toward INC-5.2 in 2025, the Chair and member states face the major task of bridging the remaining divides and reaching consensus on a number of core issues. The agreement that the "Chair's

---

[11] "Provisions governing treaty amendment vary across international environmental agreements, although it is common to provide that Parties will make every effort to reach agreement on proposed amendments by consensus, and to specify a majority decision threshold if all efforts at consensus have been exhausted. For instance, under the Minamata Convention on Mercury, Stockholm Convention, and Rotterdam Convention, treaty text amendments are adopted by consensus, or if consensus fails, a three-fourths majority of Parties present and voting at a Conference of the Parties (COP); annex adoption and amendment is considered specifically with dedicated provisions covering the adoption and amendment of annexes in each instrument. The recently adopted Convention on the Law of the Sea on the Conservation and Sustainable Use of Marine Biodiversity Beyond National Jurisdiction provides that the COP shall make every effort to adopt decisions by consensus, and that if all efforts to reach consensus have been exhausted, decisions on questions of substance (such as treaty amendments) require a two-thirds majority of the Parties present and voting" (Article 47).

Text" would be adopted as a basis for future discussions, combined with the alignment of a growing group of nations around some high ambition positions in Busan, offers a foundation for optimism. Ensuring that the treaty effectively protects human health and the environment, is adequately and reliably financed, and with effective means of decision-making and adjustment, including in response to the best available science ongoingly, will be crucial to achieving a robust and equitable agreement. Despite the challenges ahead, the determination and ambition displayed by a growing group of nations provide hope that a comprehensive treaty addressing plastic pollution is within reach despite the challenging geopolitical environment in which the negotiations will conclude and the significant economic interests in play.

Following finalization of the treaty text, next steps will be preparations for a Diplomatic Conference of Plenipotentiaries, at which time the text will be open for signature and decisions on any interim work to take place, ahead of the first Conference of the Parties (COP1). The period between finalization of the treaty text and COP1 is not yet clear and will depend in part on the timing for the treaty's coming into force, which in turn depends on the agreed number of signatories ratifying the instrument. It is estimated that it may be two, three, or more years between finalization of the initial treaty text and entry into force, placing any major decisions that are slated for COP1 to 2028 or beyond. Based on the current draft text, it appears that many substantive decisions may indeed be deferred to decision at that first meeting, meaning that decisions made at the Diplomatic Conference on the work that is to take place in the interim period will also be critical to ensuring continuation of any necessary science and technical work that will inform key decisions at COP1.

Margaret Spring, JD, joined the Monterey Bay Aquarium in 2013 to oversee its conservation and science programs, the Seafood Watch and other global sustainable seafood initiatives, as well as its science and research activities, including the Monterey Bay Aquarium Research

Institute (MBARI). From 2009 to 2013, she held leadership roles in the National Oceanic and Atmospheric Administration (NOAA). She also led The Nature Conservancy's California coastal and marine program. From 1999 to 2007, she served in the US Congress as senior counsel, then general counsel, to the Senate Committee on Commerce, Science, and Transportation. She serves on the board of the California Ocean Science Trust, is Chair of the International Science Council Expert Group on Plastic Pollution, and chaired the National Academies of Sciences, Engineering and Medicine's (NASEM) Committee on United States Contributions to Global Ocean Plastic Waste. She was a member of the Minderoo-Monaco Commission on Plastics and Human Health. She served on the Ocean Studies Board of the National Research Council (2014–2020) and was founding board member of the Monterey Bay Fisheries Trust. From 1992 to 1999, she was an environmental attorney at Sidley & Austin in Washington, DC. She is a graduate of Duke University Law School and Dartmouth College.

Cindy Matuch is a marine scientist with expertise in science-policy engagement and environmental governance. From 2023 to 2025, she was a Science Policy Fellow at the Monterey Bay Aquarium, where she worked on plastic pollution policy and science-based advocacy. In 2025, she was selected as a John A. Knauss Marine Policy Fellow through the National Oceanic and Atmospheric Administration (NOAA) Sea Grant Program, serving in the Legislative branch. Matuch holds a bachelor's degree in marine science from California State University, Monterey Bay (CSUMB) and a master's degree in Coastal Science and Policy from the University of California, Santa Cruz (UCSC).

Part 5

Joining Religious Commitments

9. A Moral Roadmap for Ending the Global Plastics Crisis

Rev. Mitchell C. Hescox

While other chapters in this book focus on medical and scientific arguments for eliminating plastics, and the theological chapters uplift the moral case for ending plastic waste, this chapter moves more toward the praxis—how do we first accept the knowledge and turn it into a moral argument that drives public opinion, leading to policy and individual behavior change for reduced plastic use and eventual elimination? To accomplish this goal, we must not make the mistake of some environmental movements. The "Big Green Groups" have accomplished much and led to significant changes in environmental laws and rising awareness among many demographic segments in the United States. However, they have failed to secure total victory on concerns such as climate change and newly identified threats such as plastic pollution.

Since I have been directly involved in defending God's creation—for at least the last decade and a half plus—environmental organizations have attempted to create a "big tent" movement that incorporates everyone. Unfortunately, they tend to engage the public with progressive values and fail to realize that at least fifty percent of the United States is not progressive and generally reacts negatively to progressive values.

For example, several years ago, I was graciously invited to a retreat organized by significant "Green Groups." As the retreat's facilitator started his presentation and outlined his goals for the retreat, his first question was: "How do we get more progressives to vote for climate change action?" I immediately reacted, saying that this is the wrong question. How do we get more conservatives to support environmental policies? Conservatives, especially conservative people of faith, represent at least fifty percent of

Americans and vote at a higher percentage than their percentage of the general population.[1]

While it will take years to analyze the 2024 American Presidential Election, I am confident that the results will show that conservative voters again voted at a higher percentage than the actual population as they were more highly motivated by the messaging of one candidate than the core supporters of the other candidate. With the American populace being more conservative than progressive, it is not surprising that any environmental concern, from plastics to climate change, continues to be a polarizing issue.

The failure to recognize that values are the driving force behind these differing political approaches is exacerbating the issue. Most attempts to mobilize Americans for a plastic-free future utilize language and value appeals that are inconsistent with conservatives' core values. In short, we need a multi-messaging effort to contact each demographic profile. Jonathan Haidt's *The Righteous Mind: Why Good People Are Divided by Politics and Religion* provides insights into how people formulate their moral foundations.[2]

Haidt's research on moral frames compares favorably to my experience using messages geared toward the evangelical community. These frames, tested in over three thousand presentations in churches, town halls, and Christian colleges around the nation, have been used to drive our education, resulting in over five million pro-life evangelical Christians acting on various environmental and public health concerns over the past five years. A few of the policy successes accomplished by our community, or where our community support had a significant influence, include the Endangered Species Act, the Mercury and Air Toxic Standard, the Great

---

[1] See Michael O. Emerson, "Christian Voters Will Play an Outsized Role in the US Election," Rice University's Baker Institute for Public Policy, September 17, 2024, doi.org/10.25613/TG0Y-VV96.

[2] Jonathan Haidt, *The Righteous Mind: Why Good People Are Divided by Politics and Religion* (Pantheon Books, 2012).

America Outdoors Act, the Inflation Reduction Act, and the New Source Methane Standard for the Oil and Gas Industry.

Attempting to prove scientific findings and pushing for government-based solutions as the primary goal remains problematic for the evangelical Christian community and American conservatives in general. Public messages using progressive-leaning language will not successfully build support for eliminating plastics. For achieving success, multiple messages from numerous trusted community members will be needed. The best analogy I can offer is that we do not need one "big tent" but a series of smaller tents raised with community-specific messaging that will join at the top and appear as one.

The Moral Roadmap

The moral roadmap that I propose lists six straightforward concepts that outline a model for building awareness, lifestyle changes, policy action, and successful outcomes in securing solutions to address plastic pollution and/or other environmental health concerns. These six steps include:

1. *Authentic Messenger*. The best messenger is always a community member. For example, an atheist trying to move a Southern Baptist church is not the best idea.
2. *The Concern*. It is necessary to identify the problem in language consistent with one's community values. Children's health, both born and unborn, remains the most important concern of evangelicals. One of the primary reasons we always discuss values in medical language and rarely use scientific terms is that medical professionals are more valued than scientists.
3. *Moral or Theological Value*. For the evangelical community, what has value is the Christian Bible.
4. *Individual Action*. Individual action is the prelude to total engagement. It is the "on ramp" to more sustained engagement. Examples include no longer using plastic food storage or containers for reheating foods (off-

gassing), using reusable grocery shopping bags, or organizing a trash/plastic clean-up along highways, parks, or waterways.
5. *Advocacy.* The more people understand that through their actions alone they cannot solve environmental problems caused by pollution, the more they are willing to work systemically with policymakers on the local, state, federal, or international levels.
6. *Hope.* If we always share dreaded consequences to our actions or inaction, it is easy for the most committed to walk away and say, "Why, bother?" What helps is to always dream about what good can happen, especially using the value systems of that community.

Because of their complexity, the remainder of this chapter will discuss points two and three of this moral roadmap. Both this model and the emphasis on value-based messaging come from my experience within the evangelical community. Hopefully, these examples will inspire readers to develop examples pertinent to their communities and raise their "tents" striving to address and hopefully solving the plastic pollution crisis.

These concepts and messages have proven successful among the most conservative demographic in the United States: evangelical Christians. The core values that help evangelicals understand and act by relying on their core values are derived from over seventeen years of experience in the evangelical community as the President/CEO and then President Emeritus of the Evangelical Environmental Network, and the successes that were achieved.

The Concern

Before exploring the best value-based approach, we must go back in time and understand why so many people outside the evangelical world never attempted to reach evangelicals and considered this portion of the population a "lost cause." Even before the Cuyahoga River's 1969 fire (the river first caught fire in 1868),[3] which became the poster child of the environmental crisis and led to the creation of the Environmental Protection Agency (EPA) in 1970, Lynn White, Jr., professor at the University of California Los Angeles, penned "The Historical Roots of Our Ecological Crisis."[4] White's essay essentially blames Christianity and dominion theology as the root evil for not caring for the earth.

As we read in the biblical book of Genesis, "Then God said, 'Let Us make man in Our image, according to Our likeness; let them have dominion over the fish of the sea, over the birds of the air, and over the cattle, over all the earth and over every creeping thing that creeps on the earth."[5] While many Christians did, and some still misinterpret this passage as giving ultimate authority to do anything to the Earth, White's paper reinforced the evangelical perception that environmentalists are anti-Bible, anti-God, tree-worshiping atheists, and thus in direct opposition to core evangelical Christian beliefs. In response to White, Dr. Francis Schaeffer gave a series of lectures at Wheaton College in 1969 that became the book *Pollution and the Death of Man*.[6] Unfortunately, Schaeffer's efforts never got much acceptance outside the evangelical higher education, even though years later, Schaeffer became the leading theologian who underpinned and co-founded the Moral Majority Movement.[7]

Change has happened and is still happening, but there remains the perception that caring for the environment (creation care) is a liberal agenda and, therefore, ungodly. Below is an example shared a few years ago by an Evangelical Environment Network supporter. While this discussion

---

[3] See Lorraine Boissoneault, "The Cuyahoga River Caught Fire at Least a Dozen Times, but No One Cared Until 1969," *Smithsonian Magazine* (2019), www.smithsonianmag.com/history/cuyahoga-river-caught-fire-least-dozen-times-no-one-cared-until-1969-180972444/.

[4] See Lynn White, Jr., "The Historical Roots of Our Ecologic Crisis," *Science* 155, no. 3767 (1967): 1203–1207.

[5] Genesis 1:26 (KJV).

[6] See Francis A. Schaeffer, *Pollution and the Death of Man* (Tyndale House, 1970).

[7] See William Edgar, "Francis Schaeffer and His Global Influence," *Westminster Magazine* 3, no. 2 (2023): wm.wts.edu/magazine-articles/francis-schaeffer-and-his-global-influence.

revolved around climate change, the principles also apply to ending the plastic crisis.

>Yesterday, I had an experience that was simultaneously strange and emblematic of encountering fellow Evangelical Christians on the issue of climate change. The context of the situation was our town's monthly "First Friday" event, staged from April through October in Warrenton, VA, to stage a block party between 5:00 and 9:00 p.m. Local craft and food vendors and civic organizations set up booths along the street to advertise and sell their products or to publicize their organizations and causes. For the past several years, we have participated in "First Friday." While operating the booth, I engaged a local pastor in conversation over climate change. The man leads a well-established local congregation, and as we entered a conversation, he resorted to many of the highly predictable tropes of climate change denial, e.g., "the science isn't settled," "there's no consensus," "it's a liberal political plot," "God granted us dominion over Creation," and "the oceans aren't warming." On each point, I summoned substantial and substantive reference to either publicly verifiable empirical data or actual reference to Scripture to counter his propositions. At that point, he would immediately move on to the next denial trope without any rebuttal to the response I'd given him. But when we got to the matter of the warming oceans, why they are warming, the role that warming plays in modifying global climate patterns, and the mountain of empirical data that directly and unequivocally links this warming to the rise in atmospheric greenhouse gases resulting from increasing consumption of hydrocarbon fuels, things started down a path into certifiable weirdness. At first, he flatly denied the cause of the atypical rise in ocean temperature as a thoroughly-documented, unnatural phenomenon with more than nearly seventy years of direct observations correlating it to a commensurate rise in atmospheric CO2 that is further correlated to increased hydrocarbon fuel consumption, i.e., a verifiable "given 'A,' then 'B,' then 'C'" chain of observation leading to causation. He then demonstrated no understanding of the relationship between climate and weather, citing that it was "hot" when he visited Africa and "it's always been hot in Africa," so there was no truth to what I just told him

regarding what we're seeing in the oceans and the linkage to what we're seeing play out in climate. Then, as I had to busy myself with other tasks at the booth, he delivered his final assessment that, contrary to what he just asserted, the oceans are warming. Still, the cause is that Hell is expanding, heating the oceans, and he could factually substantiate that from Scripture.

Some have asserted that simply being more winsome and compelling in communicating scientific information is the key to overcoming environmental threats in the United States. However, as exemplified in the story from our grassroots champion, this assumes that science is well-understood by the general population and that scientific evidence has an equally weighted value in our decision-making processes. However, that supposition is not correct for many in the evangelical community.

Instead, reframing plastic pollution within an existing moral framework and adding individual action helps to engage a much wider audience.[8] When solutions are presented as involving multiple sectors and actions and are framed according to existing values and priorities, many previously disengaged individuals willingly engage and act. Change depends on engaging existing faith and moral frameworks. These frameworks must include children's health (both unborn and born), the potential harm to future generations, business opportunities, efficient limited government action, and hope. Solutions must also include practical and meaningful individual engagement.[9] Sanctity (the sacredness of life) and purity (morally untainted) are the top moral values for the conservative evangelical community (Figure 1). Therefore, meaningful communication and education in our community must focus on these

---

[8] See Christopher Wolsko, Hector Ariceaga, and Jesse Seiden, "Red, White, and Blue Enough to Be Green: Effects of Moral Framing on Climate Change Attitudes and Conservation Behaviors," *Journal of Experimental Social Psychology* 65 (2016): 7–19.
[9] See Matthew Feinberg and Robb Willer, "The Moral Roots of Environmental Attitudes," *Psychological Science* 24, no. 1 (2012): 56–62.

two primary concerns—the best and most common messages for our community.

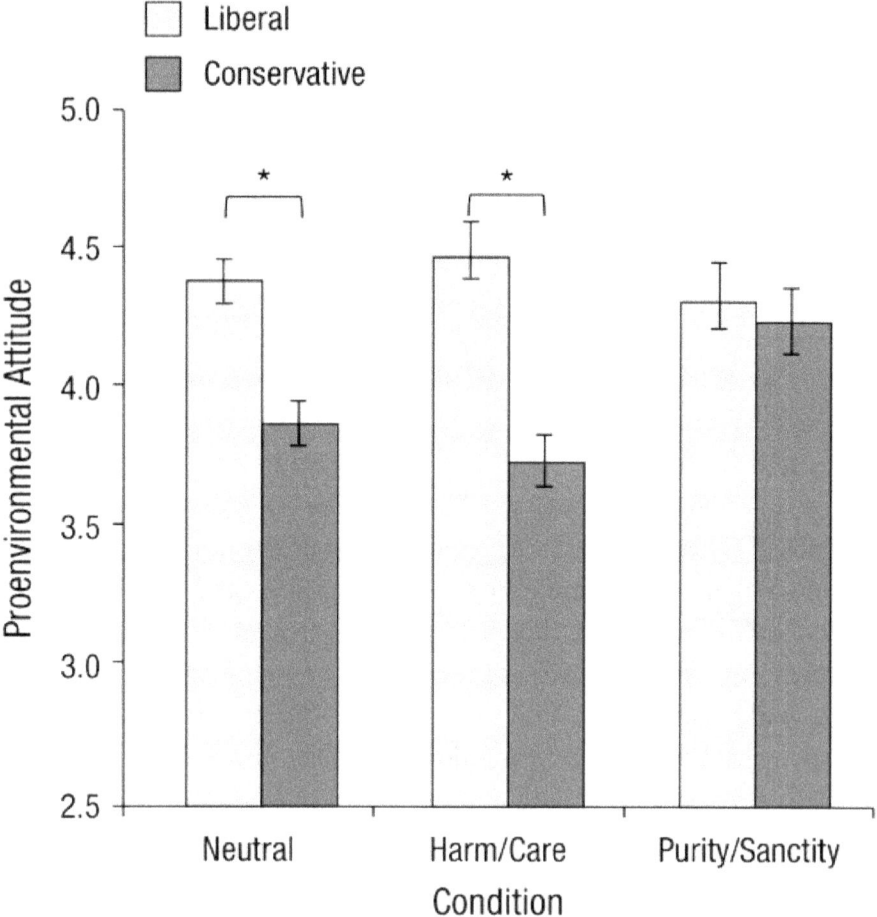

Figure 1. "Results from Study 3: mean pro-environmental attitude as a function of moral-messaging condition and political ideology (liberal = 1 SD below the mean; conservative = 1 SD above the mean). Asterisks indicate significant differences between groups (p < .001). Error bars represent ±1 SEM." Matthew Feinberg and Robb Willer, "The Moral Roots of Environmental Attitudes," *Psychological Science* 24, no. 1 (2012): 60.

For Schaeffer, "Modern man [*sic*] has been upsetting the balance of nature, and the problem is drastic and urgent. It is not just a matter of aesthetics, nor is the problem only future; the quality of life has already diminished for many modern men."[10]

Most people find a balance in life by trying to maintain stability in work, family, values, and faith, whether healthy or not. Individuals change only when their everyday life balance and values are impacted in such a way as to force a tipping point; changes are only initiated and actions taken as issues touch the center of our being and whom we care about the most.[11] When problems like plastic pollution arise, it is very easy to dismiss or deny them because they add another stressor to our hectic everyday lives.

Using the concepts first developed by Dr. Murray Bowen (1913–1990) in his Family Systems Theory, instead of being dismissive we can create a plan to recognize the key values that can potentially move individuals to act. In particular,

> Bowen family systems theory is a theory of human behavior that views the family as an emotional unit and uses systems thinking to describe the unit's complex interactions. It is the nature of a family that its members are intensely connected emotionally. Often people feel distant or disconnected from their families, but this is more feeling than fact. Families so profoundly affect their members' thoughts, feelings, and actions that it often seems as if people are living under the same "emotional skin." People solicit each other's attention, approval, and support, and they react to each other's needs, expectations, and upsets. This connectedness and reactivity make the functioning of family members interdependent. A change in one person's functioning is predictably followed by reciprocal changes in the functioning of others. Families differ somewhat in their degree of interdependence, but it is always present to some degree.[12]

---

[10] Schaeffer, *Pollution and the Death of Man*, 21.
[11] See the Bowen Center, www.thebowencenter.org.
[12] The Bowen Center for the Study of the Family, "Introduction to the Eight Concepts," www.thebowencenter.org/introduction-eight-concepts.

Taking Family Systems Theory to the next step, in 1985 Rabbi Edwin Friedman (1932–1996) wrote *Generation to Generation: Family Process in Church and Synagogue*.[13] In this seminal work, Friedman shows how churches, other faith organizations, and communities may act as systems and behave like families. For Friedman, this approach explains how a herd mentality functions within faith communities and helps us understand how we can identify the correct moral message to engage and see minds and attitudes change to create a healthy future.[14]

While many people experience and recognize environmental concerns, the evangelical community best relates to these concerns by understanding the increased harm to our children's health, both born and unborn. When threats are brought into our living rooms and our lives, we accept reality. That is why the work of Philip Landrigan and colleagues, in publishing "The Minderoo-Monaco Commission on Plastics and Human Health,"[15] provides the medical research that allows us to take the impacts and threats of plastic pollution into living rooms, schools, and physicians' offices. We encourage studying this report and learning about all the potential threats.

On Human Life

Evangelical Christians believe that all human life is sacred, that each person conceived is of equal and innate value and dignity, and that all human life is worthy of protection. Unfortunately, many in our community have viewed pro-life as only protecting the unborn child from termination. However, times are changing, and many in the evangelical community—

---

[13] See Edwin H. Friedman, *Generation to Generation: Family Process in Church and Synagogue* (Guilford Press, 1985).

[14] Family Systems Theory contains much more than the few isolated concepts presented. I was trained in Family Systems Theory during my seminary training and used Bowen and Friedman's work during my eighteen years as a local church pastor.

[15] See Philip J. Landrigan, Hervé Raps, Maureen Cropper, Caroline Bald, Manuel Brunner, Elvia Maya Canonizado, et al., "The Minderoo-Monaco Commission on Plastics and Human Health," *Annals of Global Health* 89, no. 1 (2023): 1–215.

including the National Association of Evangelicals, Focus on the Family, the Evangelical Environmental Network, and others—now understand pro-life as including life from conception to natural death, a theology much more in-tune with sound biblical teaching than only preventing a procedure from ending a pregnancy. Each child has the *right to fulfill their God-given potential,* what Jesus called the "abundant life."[16] Jesus referred to a spiritual connection and a holistic understanding of well-being, body and spirit together. He was especially concerned about vulnerable populations being denied abundant life. "Jesus said, 'Let the little children come to me, and do not hinder them, for the kingdom of heaven belongs to such as these.'"[17] My commitment to Jesus compels efforts to educate Christians to do all to defend children from life-altering and life-threatening plastic pollution. This is a pro-life concern, plain and simple.

While understanding pro-life as an all-of-life concern, the most substantial value-based messaging to address plastic pollution remains focused on the unborn and newly born child. The medical conditions that so far resonate best in our community are premature birth, cognitive disorders, preterm birth, and childhood cancers associated with living within a five-mile radius of a shell-gas fracking site. Moreover, driving interest and support on recent scientific research depend on concerns about the lowest male fertility rates in the Western world, male reproductive congenital disabilities, developmental disorders, and preterm birth associated with micro- and nano-plastics.

Sola Scriptura

Evangelicals take the Bible seriously and believe in Jesus Christ as Savior and Lord. The term "evangelical" comes from the Greek word *euangelion*, meaning "the good news" or the "gospel." Thus, the evangelical faith focuses on the "good news" of salvation brought to sinners by Jesus

---

[16] John 10:10 (NRSUE).
[17] Matthew 19:14 (NIV).

Christ.¹⁸ British historian David Bebbington provides a helpful summary of distinctive evangelical beliefs by identifying four primary characteristics of evangelicalism: primary authority of the Bible, cross-centered (a stress on the sacrifice of Jesus Christ on the cross as making possible the redemption of humanity), conversion (the belief that lives need to be transformed through a "born-again" experience and a lifelong process of following Jesus), and activism (getting busy in advancing the cause of Christ). This approach frames corporate and individual evangelism as well as moral and social reform.¹⁹

Considering the above definitions, one can see why life values and children's health are the value-based keys to opening the door to addressing creation care (Christian Environmentalism) in general and plastic pollution in particular. However, the Bible remains the foundational text. Throughout the history of Protestantism, and especially in its evangelical wing, the Bible has always been our primary rule of faith. *Sola Scriptura* (Latin for 'by scripture alone') remains our central theological statement. Since Martin Luther (1483–1546), all Christians have had open access to the Bible. While doctrine, tradition, experience, and scholarship play essential roles depending on individual denominations or congregations, sharing Scripture's concern for creation care is paramount. At the same time, admitting that biblical interpretations can cause chaos, the Bible remains the basis for life in Christ. However, biblical knowledge among US evangelicals remains woefully lacking, and this biblical illiteracy and many misinterpretations have made the efforts of groups like the Evangelical Environmental Network and others often painstakingly slow.

Some time ago, I led a community men's morning Bible study in a conservative area of the United States. The teaching was based on a passage from the letter to the Colossians:

---

[18] See National Association of Evangelicals, www.nae.org/what-is-an-evangelical/.

[19] See "Bebbington's Four Points of Evangelicalism," www.ligonier.org/posts/bebbingtons-four-points-evangelicalism.

> For in him all things were created: things in heaven and on earth, visible and invisible, whether thrones or powers or rulers or authorities; all things have been created through him and for him. He is before all things, and in him all things hold together. And he is the head of the body, the church; he is the beginning and the firstborn from among the dead, so that in everything he might have the supremacy. For God was pleased to have all his fullness dwell in him, and through him to reconcile to himself all things, whether things on earth or things in heaven, by making peace through his blood, shed on the cross.[20]

Because "for in him all things were created: things in heaven and on earth, visible and invisible, whether thrones or powers or rulers or authorities; all things have been created through him and for him," Christians are not the owners of the Earth. The Earth, God's creation, was formed by and for God, by and for Jesus. Unfortunately, too many Christians, especially evangelicals, do not understand the imperative to "work it and take care of it [the Earth]."[21]

As a case in point, immediately after sharing my thoughts and during a time set aside for reflection and discussion, one gentleman said, "I've read the Bible all my life, and I never saw this Scripture in the light of caring for the earth."

Humanity has been given a precious gift, a planet that can provide for all our needs if we only follow God and use it wisely. The same applies to the whole creation just as we are called to love our neighbor, not subjugate them. Never does the Bible support the Earth being trashed or misused. Genesis states just the opposite. The earth supplies the necessities for biological life; God designed creation for this purpose. God created and was the first gardener. For life to prosper, humans are to empower the garden to flourish. As made in God's image, we have been responsible for reflecting God's presence by caring for creation.

---

[20] Colossians 1:16–20 (NIV).
[21] Genesis 2:15 (NIV).

The sad reality is that our stewardship reflects our relationship with God. Upon a close reading of Genesis chapter 3, we understand that original sin was the temptation to be God-like, to be in control. Looking back at human history, our principal failing always seems to be the desire to be in charge, combined with the inability to live within God-given limits. The Genesis account describes a universal order with God as the loving and very good creator, humans cast in God's image as partners in maintaining creation, and all creation living sustainably.

However, our desire to be in control breaks the order, attempts to bypass the limits, and injures our relationship with God, leading to a broken and unsustainable world. Each time we use more than we need or consume more than our share, we perpetuate our brokenness, support our vanity, and continue disregarding God's limits. This behavior distorts the creation and impacts all.

Throughout the Hebrew Scriptures, God defines and provides deliberate instructions for tending the Earth. Although many Christians have not yet made the connection, the Bible offers definitive mandates to live in a reciprocal relationship with the non-human creation. The biblical books of Deuteronomy, Numbers, and Leviticus, God explicitly instruct to observe a Sabbath rest for the land, to implement crop rotation and animal husbandry. There are strict ordinances regarding farming, livestock management, and land use. These conditions define the parameters for living in a relationship with God, people, and the Earth in an integrated approach to abundant life. One of the most illustrative passages stresses that "the land shall not be sold in perpetuity, for the land is mine; with me you are but aliens and tenants. Throughout the land that you hold, you shall provide for the redemption of the land."[22]

However, ownership is not the primary biblical concern; it is people, especially those marginalized or on the fringes of society. I mention just a couple of passages to illustrate these commands. First, "Defend the weak and the fatherless; uphold the cause of the poor and the oppressed. Rescue

---

[22] Leviticus 25:23–24 (NRSVUE).

the weak and the needy."[23] Second, "He will reply, 'Truly I tell you, whatever you did not do for one of the least of these, you did not do for me.'"[24]

The Bible calls us to defend life and empower life to the fullest by following Jesus's commands. Yet, we have failed to understand that plastic pollution significantly impacts humanity. Overcoming our failure requires a renewed study of Scripture to grasp the critical importance of creation care as discipleship. As John Stott (1921–2011), one of the great evangelical leaders of the twentieth and early twenty-first century, wrote in his last book, *The Radical Disciple: Some Neglected Aspects of Our Calling*, creation care is one of the "neglected aspects of our calling."[25]

The Moral Roadmap Works

The best way to convey environmental threats is by stressing threats to *our children*, at least within the evangelical community and with other social conservatives in the United States. Unfortunately, discussing global threats or environmental health issues results in a cognitive disconnect. People might give a few dollars to feed a child in Africa, Asia, or South America. However, for most in the United States, their behavior will neither change nor result in advocating for environmental policies or corporate changes— all things are truly local.

Below is an example of a presentation in a Southern Baptist Church in Alabama during the first administration of President Donald J. Trump (2017–2021). This is a true story that has been repeated hundreds of times in our ministry while the evening's discussion centered on climate change; it could be any environmental health concern that threatens children.

During the first Trump Administration, I was invited to speak at a weeknight gathering at Southern Baptist Church. Attendance was

---

[23] Psalm 82:3–4 (NIV).
[24] Matthew 25:45 (NIV).
[25] John R. W. Stott, *The Radical Disciple: Some Neglected Aspects of Our Calling* (InterVarsity Press, 2010).

between 100 and 125; the attendees were local church members, students from a local Christian College, and their professors. However, one attendee stood out. She was a mature woman with elaborately coiffed hair, numerous gold chains around her neck, and wearing a red skirt-suit with the jacket adorned front and back with at least 100 pins showing her support for President Trump. My mind was spinning. Was this going to be an evening dominated by debunked theories? Would this woman attempt to take over the meeting? I took a deep breath, prayed, and dived into my talk. To my surprise, the woman seemed to listen intently to my presentation, track and follow the discussion during our open dialogue, and take it all in. Being extremely curious, I walked over to her as the evening ended. "I'm surprised to see you here this evening; you are a great supporter of President Trump, and he denied the reality of climate change." She just looked up at me in an assured, steady voice and said, "I'm sure no one has ever talked to President Trump the way you talked, and if you could talk to him, you would change his mind."

In another similar account, several Evangelical Environmental Network staff were invited to present at a conference on Gulf Coast restoration near Mobile. The night before the conference, the leadership asked the presenters to share a meal with key attendees. A good Southern Baptist attendee scrimmaged with us over our changing climate during the dinner. He was adamant that climate change was a liberal deception and that the science was far from settled. Needless to say, the dinner discussion was, at best, tenuous, if not outright hostile. To our surprise, the gentleman still attended the next day's seminar and carefully listened as we shared our hearts on how fossil fuel pollution harms our children's lungs, hearts, minds, and lives. Immediately after my talk, he walked up to me and asked if climate change was responsible for all these children's health threats. "No," I replied, "but the same fossil fuels that are harming our children cause climate change." "Okay, he said. I want to defend our kids!"

The above examples show what the moral roadmap that I proposed can accomplish with conservative evangelical Christians. These same evangelicals, once committed and passionate, can make a difference in public policy. While the Evangelical Environmental Network could share hundreds of examples, one of my favorite narratives centers on the late Senator John S. McCain, III (1936–2018). Although I met with the Senator several times, I cannot say I knew him beyond his gruff demeanor and no-nonsense attitude. However, one day, I got a brief smile when I asked him to sign my copy of his 1999 book, *Faith of My Fathers*.[26] However, what sealed my admiration for the Senator was his decision to vote against the 2017 Congressional Review Act (CRA), which kept the Bureau of Land Management Methane Standard in place to limit fugitive pollutants on natural wells on public lands.[27] There were multiple reasons for his vote, but according to the Senator's staff, one very important factor was over fourteen thousand Arizona evangelicals (organized by the Evangelical Environmental Network) asking him to stop the CRA to benefit children's health.

Concluding Thoughts

Often, I am asked what the most significant environmental health concern is today. My usual reply starts with a statement from the *Lancet* Commission on Climate Change and Human Health, "Climate change is the most significant global health threat facing the world in the 21st century, but it is also the most incredible opportunity to redefine the social and environmental determinants of health."[28] Plastic pollution is a close second, for me, after climate change, because plastic pollution may result in life-altering changes in our genetic makeup, including our ability to reproduce. Hence, the first good news is that if we end our addiction to fossil fuels, we can reduce both threats to human health.

The second good news is that we can solve these crises but not without the support of conservatives and conservative people of faith. The major

---

[26] John McCain with Marc Salter, *Faith of My Fathers* (Random House, 1999).
[27] See www.gao.gov/legal/congressional-review-act.
[28] "The *Lancet* Countdown on Health and Climate," www.thelancet.com/countdown-health-climate.

environmental organizations have significantly reduced pollution and made tremendous gains in environmental health. However, in the past two decades, the polarization of the American people has diminished the attention given to these issues among conservative citizens and conservative policymakers. Only by utilizing value-based messaging and tools like the moral roadmap will the final goals be reached in defending human health and restoring a healthy planet.

The simple beauty of the moral roadmap is that it can be adapted for use with any demographic segment only by knowing a group's values and the authoritative basis for their values. It is time to adopt solutions for plastic pollution and other environmental threats. This chapter offers new ways to address environmental concerns and attempts new approaches to generate support across demographics. Past efforts simply have finalized on the work to be done, and we all know that doing the same thing over and over again will not result in a different answer.

To conclude, in the letter to the Romans we read, "May the God of hope fill you with all joy and peace as you trust in him, so that you may overflow with hope by the power of the Holy Spirit."[29]

The Rev. Mitchell C. Hescox serves as a climate and energy policy consultant and is the President Emeritus of the Evangelical Environmental Network (EEN), where he led the EEN team for fifteen years. He co-authored *Caring for Creation: The Evangelical Guide to Climate Change and a Healthy Environment* with nationally known meteorologist Paul Douglas. He also contributed to *Sacred Acts: How Churches Are Working Together to Protect Earth's Climate*; *Health of People, Health of Planet, Our Responsibility*; and *Loving the Least of These*. He has testified before Congress, spoken at the White House, and presented at the Vatican and the Council for Foreign Relations. He has appeared on CNN, NPR, PRI,

---

[29] Romans 15:13 (NIV).

MSNBC, BBC, and numerous radio programs, both Christian and secular. Rev. Hescox and EEN have been widely recognized for their advocacy for the Mercury and Air Toxics Standard (MATS), Land Water Conservation Fund (LWCF), Growing Climate Solutions Act, Infrastructure Investment and Jobs Act, the Inflation Reduction Act, and Methane Leakage Reduction Standards, among others. He is a member of the National Association of Evangelicals, a past member of the National Association of Evangelicals (NAE) Board of Directors, a past member of Environmental Protection Agency (EPA) Clean Air Act Advisory Committee, the Pennsylvania Department of Environmental Protection's Citizen Advisory Council, and a member of the American Academy of Arts and Sciences' Commission on Accelerating Climate Action. Before joining EEN, he pastored a local church for 18 years, and before the call to ordained ministry served the coal and utility industry as Director, Fuel Systems for Allis Mineral Systems (York, PA).

10. A Message from Judaism

Rabbi Leonid Feldman

I believe that the idea of joining science and theology in the struggle to end plastic pollution is very appropriate. In chapter two of the Book of Genesis, at the very beginning of the Bible, we read "The Lord God took the man and placed him in the Garden of Eden, to till it and tend it." This verse is one of many in the Bible which clearly express God's concern for preserving nature. It is obvious that all the great crises confronting humanity today are the results of human choices and the consequences of human actions.

A fundamental concept in Judaism, which has become very well-known is Tikkun Olam, which means the "Repairing of the World." It is a concept that has been mentioned by almost every American president in the last fifty years. Tikkun Olam means that we, humans, have the responsibility to work towards healing the environment and to serve as much as we can as good stewards of God's creation.

Now how does Tikkun Olam relate to plastics? The connection lies in plastics' increasingly visible harms to God's creation, in plastics' pollution of the lands and the ocean, in the harm plastics cause to whales and seabirds, and the disease, disability, and death that plastics cause in people of all ages. We cannot allow these evils to continue. We have a responsibility to intervene, to help repair this damaged world.

Each one of us must first take personal action to reduce these harms, for example, by using less plastic in our daily lives, like the plastic water bottles that we all use and just throw out, and so on. But beyond the personal, we also have a responsibility to address the dangers of plastics at a systemic, societal level, in the cities, states, provinces where we live, in our countries, and even internationally. We must work with legislators to create laws and policies that will reduce plastics' harms to human health and the environment—for example, by banning most single-use plastics and requiring manufacturers to take back and reuse plastic products.

Most importantly, we must work through the United Nations to craft a Global Plastic Treaty that protects human health and safeguards human rights by limiting global plastic production, especially the production of single-use plastics, and also addressing the thousands of toxic and unregulated chemicals in plastics.

Hence, I urge the delegates from nations around the world who will gather this year to finalize the Global Plastic Treaty to write a treaty that protects the health of all living beings, safeguards human rights, and heals our wounded world.

Rabbi Leonid Feldman is a Soviet-born American Conservative Jewish rabbi. From 2005 to 2022 he was the spiritual leader of Temple Beth El in West Palm Beach, Florida. He is the host of the podcast "Ask the Rabbi."

11. A Message from the Eastern Orthodox Church

His All-Holiness Ecumenical Patriarch Bartholomew

Distinguished organizers and esteemed participants, it is truly a privilege to address you from a distance on the vital subject of Plastic Pollution that you are discussing at Boston College on October 4–5, 2024. During your conference, entitled "Joining Science and Theology to End Plastic Pollution, Protect Health, and Advance Social Justice," you will consider numerous aspects of this challenge, including the critical relationship between science and religion in our age, as well as the urgent need to advance public health and social justice in our world.

For more than thirty years, the Ecumenical Patriarchate has underlined the imperative to preserve the natural environment, protecting its resources from destructive and detrimental chemical materials. We have also emphasized that we can only hope to resolve or expect to restrain the climate crisis with the collective and collaborative effort of all academic disciplines and social domains.

Above all, we have highlighted the intimate and essential relationship between what goes on around us and what goes on inside us. Because the way we perceive creation is the way that we will inevitably handle creation. If we appreciate our world as something ephemeral and expedient, then we will naturally treat it as something marketable and profitable. But if we approach our world as something invaluable and spiritual—that is to say, as something that we received as a gift from above and from our ancestors, but also as something we should refer to God in thanksgiving while handing down to our children in love—then we will invariably respect it as something far greater than us and our interests.

Dear friends, beyond the awareness that we must radically change our attitude and behavior, what has changed in recent years is the reaction of nature itself to our careless actions and insensitive behaviors. We have learned that not only are we inseparably interconnected as human beings, but also that what happens outside us is integrally related to what exists inside us. Not only have we polluted our oceans and our waters with plastic, but we have even compromised our health and jeopardized our brothers and sisters. Plastics no longer merely surround us; they permeate our body, pervade our population, and penetrate our planet. What we desperately need is not just cleaner products or more sustainable packaging. We need a new worldview and a new way of living. Limiting single-use plastics and avoiding over-production of plastics are important steps along a journey that leads back to the heart and its choices.

I wish you every blessing and success in your work.

Ecumenical Patriarch Bartholomew is the spiritual leader of Eastern Orthodox Christians. He has been the Patriarch of Constantinople since 1991.

12. A Message from Tibetan Buddhism

The Dalai Lama

I am pleased to send my warm greetings to participants of the conference on "Joining Science and Theology to End Plastic Pollution, Protect Health, and Advance Social Justice."

When I was growing up in Tibet, it was natural for Tibetans on the road to stop by a river when thirsty and drink water without any hesitation. Tibet then was fortunate to have a clean environment and so the purity of the river water was certain. It was only when I had to leave Tibet and in the years that passed by when I was made to understand that one should not be drinking from the rivers as they would be polluted. Over the years, in my meetings with ecologists, environmentalists, and scientists, I learned that this is a very serious matter.

Similarly, modern science informs us that something like plastic that has been useful in our daily life is also a dangerous pollutant that threatens life on this planet. All of us are the same in desiring happiness and not wanting suffering. Therefore, ignoring the negative impact of plastics and misusing them for short-term purposes is going to cost humanity greatly in the long run. From that viewpoint, the key thing is the need to have a sense of Universal Responsibility, the real source of happiness.

Also, in consideration of our future generations, we must do our best not to exploit every available thing, including plastics. With a genuine sense of universal responsibility, as the central motivation and principle, we must ensure that the direction of our relations with the environment must be well balanced.

It is also encouraging that the UN has over the years expanded its task to take on the challenge of safeguarding the long-term health of our planet and ourselves. Each and every one of us living on this planet has the responsibility to do our part. Your conference is serving a very useful purpose from this perspective in sensitizing individuals, organizations, and governments about the importance of doing away with plastic for the good of humanity.

With my prayers and good wishes for the success of the conference.

The fourteenth **Dalai Lama** is the highest spiritual leader of Tibetan Buddhism.

Part 6

Supporting Political Engagements

13. A Message from the Prince of Monaco

Albert II

I would like to thank you for your dedication to addressing the crucial issue of plastic pollution. I highly value the expertise of the individuals gathered here, the excellence of the program to which you are all committed, and the remarkable work conducted by Boston College.

Four years ago, we organized a symposium in Monaco on the interactions between ocean pollution and human health, which I believe marked a significant milestone. I am pleased to acknowledge Professor Philip Landrigan, who led that event alongside our Scientific Center of Monaco. This is why I am thrilled that you are to continue this work and to tackle this sensitive and highly urgent issue.

There is no need to remind you of the issues—six billion tons of plastic already pollute our seas, with millions more added annually. This pollution is responsible for the deaths of one million birds and over 100,000 marine mammals every year. Moreover, as plastic decomposes into microparticles, it contaminates every ecosystem and the entire food chain right up to us humans.

Yet, solutions abound—whether technical or political—and we must all engage to implement them.

I am, of course, referring first of all to the ongoing UN negotiations aimed at creating a legally-binding instrument to regulate plastic throughout its entire life cycle. This treaty would represent a major step forward closely aligned with another urgent issue, the fight against fossil fuels—a leading cause of climate change. Rest assured, Monaco remains fully committed to supporting the highest ambitions in these treaty negotiations.

However, I am also referring to local actions such as those implemented by my government in Monaco. Although these efforts are spreading globally, their pace remains frustratingly slow. The expansion of waste sorting, the promotion of recycling, the ban on single-use plastics, and the proliferation of support for alternative solutions, are tools readily available to us.

Finally, beyond these political initiatives, I would like to highlight the diversity, richness, and effectiveness of numerous actions undertaken by civil society, which are also developing worldwide. This is why through my foundation we launched the "BeMed Initiative" (*Be*yond Plastics *Med*) several years ago. BeMed supports innovative projects combating plastic pollution throughout the entire Mediterranean region. Since its inception, BeMed has supported nearly one hundred projects across fifteen different countries. Beyond financial aid, BeMed facilitates the sharing of experiences, the exchange of best practices, and the replication of effective measures, especially in avoiding plastic use.

All of these efforts demonstrate that action is both necessary and possible. Taking action, as you are doing today, has become a matter of the utmost urgency. Therefore, I can only encourage and commend you on this important initiative.

Albert II is the Prince of Monaco. He has reigned since 2005.

14. Proposing and Signing a Declaration

Karen Bullock

In March 2022, the UN Environment Assembly voted to develop a Global Plastics Treaty. Its goals are to reduce plastic pollution across the entire plastic lifecycle and safeguard human health. An Intergovernmental Negotiating Committee met several times to draft the treaty with a fifth meeting convened in the Republic of Korea in late November 2024.

The "Minderoo-Monaco Commission on Plastics and Human Health" wished to make a strong statement in advance of the Korea meeting calling for a Global Plastics Treaty that would include two key provisions: a mandatory, legally-binding global cap on the production of new plastics, and comprehensive regulation of the thousands of chemicals in plastics. The Commission considers these provisions essential for protecting human health and advancing social justice. The Commission recommended additionally that the Treaty should include restrictions on single-use plastics.

To set its conclusions and recommendations in a humanistic context, the Minderoo-Monaco Commission made the decision to convene an international conference in the run-up to the Korea meeting to examine the plastics crisis through the lenses of ethics and morality. The Commission chose to convene this conference at Boston College because a unique and distinctive aspect of Boston College's program for Global Public Health and the Common Good is its strong focus on the ethical and legal foundations of global public health.

This emphasis reflects our foundation at Boston College in the Jesuit, Catholic tradition of service to others and our commitment to a preferential option for the poor. We stand with and for those whose voices are often the last to be heard, if heard at all. In the times of need, to confront global public health challenges such as plastics pollution, which disproportionately impact marginalized individuals and low-resourced communities, our collective action is paramount.

A key goal of the 2024 Boston College conference "Joining Science and Theology to End Plastic Pollution, Protect Health, and Advance Social Justice" was to produce a Declaration at the conference conclusion that speaks to the moral and ethical dimension of the plastics crisis. This Declaration is based on the recognition that the global plastics crisis is more than an environmental crisis and more than a threat to health. It is also an ethical crisis—an affront to human dignity. Accordingly, the Declaration urges the UN negotiators to incorporate provisions into the Treaty that are explicitly designed to advance human rights and protect the world's poorest people against plastic's threats to health. The Declaration concludes with the following words:

> Continuing unchecked, increases in plastic production are unethical and immoral. They threaten all life on earth. Those who advocate for unchecked growth in plastics must re-examine their behavior, embrace the reality that the earth is a shared inheritance—a gift from the Creator, and work toward a more equitable and sustainable future. All of us have a shared responsibility to be good stewards of God's creation.

Karen Bullock, PhD, LICSW, FGSA, APHSW-C, is the Louise McMahon Ahearn Endowed Professor in the Boston College School of Social Work and in the program Global Public Health and the Common Good. She is a Licensed Independent Clinical Social Work (LICSW) with mental health practice experience and expertise in health disparities, health equity, serious illness care, aging and gerontology, hospice, palliative and end-of-life care decision making. She has served as Principal Investigator and/or Co-Investigator for over $5 million in federal grant funding focused on equity and inclusion for workforce development, aging, and health network sustainability. Dr. Bullock is a John A. Hartford Faculty

Scholar and has served on several national boards and committees, including the Social Work Hospice and Palliative Care Network (SWHPN) as vice-chair and the American Cancer Society (ACS) Oncology Social Work Research Peer Review Committee, past chair. She is a member of the National Academies of Sciences, Engineering, and Medicine (NASEM) Roundtable on Quality Care for People with Serious Illness, a board member of the Palliative Care Quality Collaborative (PCQ), Steering Committee member for the Duke University REACH Equity Center, affiliate faculty at the Center to Advance Palliative Care (CAPC), and has an appointment in the Department of Psychosocial Oncology and Palliative Care at Dana Farber Cancer Institute (DFCI).

15. Declaration: Our Shared Responsibility to End Plastic Pollution, Protect Human Health, and Advance Social Justice for All

Conference Participants

Boston College convened an international Conference on October 4–5, 2024: "Joining Science and Theology to End Plastic Pollution, Protect Health, and Advance Social Justice." Scientists, ethicists, lawyers, economists, engineers, policy makers, and religious leaders participated. This conference took place one month before the fifth and final round of negotiations for the United Nations Global Plastics Treaty. The main conclusions of the conference: Continuing unchecked increases in plastic production are unethical and immoral. Continuing increases in plastic production are responsible for damages that threaten all life on earth. Those who advocate for unchecked growth in plastics must re-examine their behavior, embrace the reality that the earth is a shared inheritance—a gift from the Creator—and work toward a more equitable and sustainable future.

Conference participants and all who have signed this Declaration urge the UN treaty negotiators to recognize that current patterns of plastic production cannot continue. We urge the negotiators to craft a treaty that prioritizes human health, safeguards the environment, and advances human rights.

The Conference adopted the following findings and recommendations:

Findings

1. *Plastics cause disease, disability, and premature death at every stage of their life cycle—in production, use, and disposal.* People who use plastics are exposed to the more than 16,000 synthetic chemicals that

are in plastics and leak out. Many of these chemicals are highly toxic. They include carcinogens, neurotoxicants, and endocrine disruptors. They are responsible for widespread human exposure and for disease in people of all ages. Workers who make plastics suffer increased rates of cancer as well as pulmonary, metabolic and neurologic diseases. Microplastic particles are linked to increased risks for heart disease, stroke, and death. The diseases caused by plastics result in annual costs of $675 billion in the USA and $1.2 trillion globally. These great costs are larger than the GDPs of many countries.

2. *Plastics endanger human reproduction.* Toxic chemicals in plastics, notably endocrine-disrupting phthalates, are associated with male reproductive birth defects. They are linked to global declines in sperm counts and to decreased human fertility. These damages threaten humanity's future.

3. *Plastics damage infants and children.* Children are at very high risk of toxic injury from plastic chemicals. Even low-level exposure can cause permanent injury. Exposures in pregnancy are especially dangerous and are linked to prematurity, stillbirth, low birth weight, birth defects, neurodevelopmental disorders and childhood leukemia.

4. *Plastic production worsens climate change.* Nearly ninety-nine percent of plastics are made from fossil fuels—crude oil, fracked gas and coal. Plastic production generates nearly two billion tons (two Gigatons) of carbon dioxide and other greenhouse gases each year—more than the annual emissions of Brazil.

5. *Plastics threaten human rights.* Plastics' harms are unjustly distributed. Groups at increased risk include: people of color, Indigenous populations, fossil fuel extraction workers, chemical and plastic production workers, informal waste and recovery workers,

and persons living in communities near plastic production facilities. The disproportionate exposures of these vulnerable populations are immoral. They are environmental injustices. They are violations of human rights.

6. *Plastic recycling does not work.* Only seven to eight percent of plastic is recycled. Despite much effort, plastic recycling lags far behind paper, glass, and aluminum recycling and is not improving. The problem is not careless behavior by individuals. The problem lies with plastics themselves. Plastics are complex, they contain multiple toxic chemicals, and they resist recycling. Contrary to the claims of the plastic industry, and despite much effort and investment, "advanced recycling," "chemical recycling" and "plastic pyrolysis" are failed technologies.

7. *Plastic pollution is a global threat.* Because plastic is persistent in the environment and little is recycled, nearly six billion tons of plastic waste now pollute the planet. Much is in the ocean, where it washes up on beaches, endangers whales, kills seabirds, and breaks down into microplastic particles. Microplastic particles enter the food chain and are consumed by people.

8. *Relentless increases in production are the main driver of plastic's worsening harms.* Annual plastic output has grown more than 200-fold—from two million tons in 1950 to over 400 million tons today. Half of all plastic ever made has been produced since 2000. Production is on track to double by 2040 and triple by 2060. Single-use plastic accounts for thirty-five to forty percent of current output. Its manufacture is increasing rapidly, and contributes disproportionately to plastic waste.

Recommendations

1. *Production limits*. Mandatory, legally-binding limits on production of new plastic, especially single-use plastics, with targets and timetables must be the core of the Global Plastics Treaty.

2. *Recycling is not the solution*. We cannot recycle our way out of the plastics crisis.

3. *Toxic chemicals*. The Treaty must address the thousands of chemicals in plastics. These chemicals are integral components of all plastics and cannot be excluded from the Treaty. They are responsible for much of the disease and death caused by plastics. They are poorly regulated, and many have never been tested for safety or toxicity. The Treaty must set strict standards for all chemicals in plastics, requiring testing and full disclosure of information on their nature and toxicity, and banning harmful chemicals such as PFAS from food packaging and from goods designed for children.

4. *Extended Producer Responsibility*. The Treaty must mandate Extended Producer Responsibility (take-back) of all plastic products, prohibit most single-use plastics, prohibit chemical recycling in any form, and enhance the infrastructure needed to boost plastic reuse.

5. *Science*. Treaty implementation must be guided by an International Science Advisory Panel independent of the plastics industry.

6. *Funding*. Treaty implementation must be adequately funded. International funding will be required in many low- and middle-income countries.

7. *Monitoring*. Continued monitoring of plastic production, plastic pollution, plastic chemical exposures, and plastics' harms to human health will be essential. Only through transparent monitoring and independent research can progress be assessed, unintended consequences avoided, and course corrections made.

Conclusion

Plastic is not an isolated problem. Like climate change, air pollution, and escalating inequality, the plastics crisis is a social and ethical challenge. It is another example of humanity's reckless strip-mining of the earth's resources and mortgaging of our common future for short-term economic gain.

To effectively confront the plastics crisis and the other great challenges of our age, we need to develop legal and technical solutions such as the UN Global Plastics Treaty. But additionally, we must at a deeper level reexamine our relationships with each other and with the earth. We must recognize that we are all connected with one other and with the planet. All of us, and especially those who lead governments, international organizations, and major corporations, have a shared responsibility to be good stewards of God's creation. We need to embrace a new approach that transforms our way of living in the world, our lifestyles, our relationship with the earth's resources, and generally how we look at humanity and all life. Such an approach is essential if we wish to leave a habitable planet for our children, our children's children, and the generations yet to come.

Conclusion

16. A Manual for Moral Collectives: Our Shared Responsibility to End Plastic Pollution, Protect Human Health, and Advance Social Justice for All

James F. Keenan, SJ

In many ways this volume is the result of two volumes already published by the strikingly indefatigable pair of Public Health Professor Philip Landrigan and Theological Ethicist Andrea Vicini: *Ethical Challenges in Global Public Health: Climate Change, Pollution, and the Health of the Poor* and *The Rising Global Cancer Pandemic: Health, Ethics, and Social Justice*.[1] These two volumes set the stage for these scholars to face with other esteemed colleagues the specific challenge of global plastic pollution.

At Boston College, Landrigan is Director of the Program for Global Public Health and the Common Good, and Director of the Global Observatory on Planetary Health. From 2015 to 2018, he co-chaired the *Lancet* Commission on Pollution and Health, which found that pollution is responsible for an estimated nine million deaths per year, is closely linked to climate change, and is an existential threat to planetary health. Since 2019, he has chaired the Monaco Commission on Human Health and Ocean Pollution examining the links between ocean pollution and human health. From 2021 to 2023, he chaired the Minderoo-Monaco Commission on Plastics and Human Health, which examined plastics' impacts on human health across the plastic life cycle and formulated recommendations to guide drafting of the UN Global Plastics Treaty,

---

[1] See Philip J. Landrigan and Andrea Vicini, eds., *Ethical Challenges in Global Public Health: Climate Change, Pollution, and the Health of the Poor*, Global Theological Ethics in the World Church, vol. 1 (Pickwick Publications, 2021); Andrea Vicini, Philip J. Landrigan, and Kurt Straif, eds., *The Rising Global Cancer Pandemic: Health, Ethics, and Social Justice*, Global Theological Ethics in the World Church, vol. 2 (Pickwick Publications, 2022).

currently in development.² This recent position led to the conference at Boston College that this collection of essays captures.

Vicini is the Michael P. Walsh Professor of Bioethics and Chairperson of the Boston College Theology Department. He has taught in Italy, Albania, Mexico, Chad, and France and is co-chair of the international network Catholic Theological Ethics in the World Church,³ as well as a lecturer and member of associations of moral theologians and bioethicists in Italy, Europe, and the US. Vicini has been a leader in theological ethics, inviting scholars to form collectives to respond to the challenges of our times.

Like Landrigan, Vicini is a pediatrician. Together, in this collection they join Karen Bullock, the Louise McMahon Ahearn Endowed Professor in the Boston College School of Social Work and in the program on Global Public Health and Common Good. Still there is another colleague to recognize, Professor Summer Sherburne Hawkins from the Boston College School of Social Work. As the Associate Director for the Global Public Health and the Common Good program she partnered with Landrigan, Vicini, and Bullock and became the fourth member of the quadrumvirate who organized this conference. In these pages together they provide us a way of participating in the attempt to overcome plastic pollution.

Their ongoing legacy is to put into the hands of like-minded scholars the fundamental resources for social change. Moreover, their aim is not primarily to engage or motivate the singular student or scholar. Rather, because collective work is so urgently needed, this manual is for a shared learning, a shared deliberation, and a shared action program to reduce plastic pollution. The individual reader is invited to find other companions so as to work collaboratively with one another to answer the call for equitable protection from the ravages of plastic pollution.

---

² See Philip J. Landrigan, Hervé Raps, Maureen Cropper, Caroline Bald, Manuel Brunner, Elvia Maya Canonizado, et al., "The Minderoo-Monaco Commission on Plastics and Human Health," *Annals of Global Health* 89, no. 1 (2023), doi.org/10.5334/aogh.4056.

³ See Catholic Theological Ethics in a World Church, www.catholicethics.com.

Therefore, do not put this manual away, rather share it with others so as to alert them and work with them to address the struggle before us. It is for this reason we publish it in an excellent online, no-cost series.

A Manual for Collectives Seeking to Overturn the Devastating Impact of Plastic Pollution

These essays provide readers with a manual to help groups move toward organizing for a social change regarding the production and use of plastics. The concluding chapter of this collection, the conference's own declaration, "Our Shared Responsibility to End Plastic Pollution, Protect Human Health, and Advance Social Justice for All," was signed by conference delegates just before the Boston College international Conference on October 4–5, 2024: "Joining Science and Theology to End Plastic Pollution, Protect Health, and Advance Social Justice," one month before the much anticipated fifth and final round of negotiations for the United Nations Global Plastics Treaty.

That session lasted until December 1st without closure and established a second meeting for the fifth resumed session from August 5–14, 2025 in Geneva, Switzerland, after the previous meeting in Busan, South Korea, ended without a final agreement.

The Declaration helpfully summarizes their eight major findings. Their first finding notes that "*Plastics cause disease, disability, and premature death at every stage of their life cycle–in production, use and disposal.*" With more than sixteen thousand synthetic chemicals that are in plastics and leak out, the cost of the diseases that they cause "result in annual costs of \$675 billion in the USA and \$1.2 trillion globally." Their last finding claims that "*Relentless increases in production are the main driver of plastic's worsening harms.*" This is because "annual plastic output has grown more than 200-fold—from two million tons in 1950 to over 400 million tons today." They add: "Production is on track to double by 2040 and triple by 2060."[4]

---

[4] See Chapter 15 in this volume.

The Declaration then makes seven notable and easy to remember recommendations from limiting production and recognizing that plastics recycling is generally ineffective to funding the treaty's implementation and subsequent monitoring. The three-page Declaration is a *Magna Carta* on the astonishing harm of plastic production.

This project and its authors want to make you capable of working with us toward subduing this global threat. Therein each of the essays provide the foundations for that collective endeavor.

Safeguarding Human Health against Plastics and Petrochemicals: A Scientific and Moral Imperative

The second chapter is without a doubt the finest collective report explaining why plastics production is so morally problematic. It is impeccably documented. With Landrigan joining a team of four members of the Minderoo Foundation and led by Sarah Dunlop, they present a dense but highly accessible essay laced with memorable phrasing that should be repeated by readers wanting to summon others in a call to respond. Here, I highlight ten of them; each of them has remarkable insights.

1. "Plastics are the signature material of our age."

2. "These harms are not equitably distributed."

3. "These groups did not create the plastics crisis. They do not profit from it. They lack the power to address it. Yet they suffer its most severe consequences. They are victims of social and environmental injustice on a planetary scale."

4. "Plastics are complex manufactured chemical materials."

5. "Plastic production is highly energy-intensive, and virtually all of the energy required for plastic manufacture comes from fossil fuel combustion."

6. "Plastic production workers, plastic waste pickers, and residents of vulnerable 'fenceline' communities living closely adjacent to production facilities suffering the most."

7. "Plastic production is associated with extreme exposures that occur during catastrophic failures of the plastic production process, such as fires and explosions, oil spills, and chemical spills."

8. "An estimated 350 million tons of plastic waste are produced globally each year, and an estimated six billion tons, seventy-five percent of all plastic ever made, pollute the planet. This waste causes extensive contamination of the environment, including the ocean, and it threatens the lives of two billion people worldwide with eleven million waste pickers lacking safe workplaces and protective equipment."

9. "Plastic recycling, known variously as chemical recycling, mechanical recycling, enhanced recycling, pyrolysis, and upcycling is highly ineffective. Despite exaggerated claims by the plastic industry about the effectiveness of recycling, less than ten percent of all plastic is recycled globally. Plastic recycling and reuse lags far behind paper, glass, and aluminum recycling. Toxic chemical content and complexity are the major impediments."

10. "Residential proximity to a landfill increases cancer risk."

Three subsequent claims merit even more attention. First, plastic chemicals are already in us. Indeed, the following claim is accompanied by six footnotes and twenty-five lines of documentation:

Plastic Chemicals Are Ubiquitous in the Human Body. Plastic chemicals are found in seminal fluid, follicular fluid, amniotic fluid, cord blood, meconium, children's and adult's blood and urine, breast milk, and hair, as well as in solid tissues such as liver, brain, breast tissue, and adipose tissue. National biomonitoring surveys detect several hundred plastic-associated chemicals in the bodies of virtually all humans of all ages.[5]

Second, they highlight the astonishingly unethical impact of governmental subsidies for plastic production:

The human health costs resulting from exposures to plastic-associated chemicals are much larger than the subsidies provided by governments to plastic producers. This creates an ethical imbalance in which plastic producers and fossil fuel corporations are rewarded economically for creating harms to health that fall disproportionately on the poorest and most vulnerable members of societies.[6]

Third, they articulate the hope of a treaty on the horizon:

The UN Environment Assembly adopted a historic resolution on March 2, 2022, to develop a global plastics treaty. The stated goal of this treaty is to reduce plastic pollution, including ocean pollution and microplastics, across the entire plastic life cycle. Treaty negotiations are on a fast track. To date, an Intergovernmental Negotiating Committee (INC) has met five times with a sixth meeting scheduled for 2025. A plastics treaty that prioritizes protection of human health will contain two key provisions—a cap on production of new plastics and strict regulation of plastic-associated chemicals. More than one hundred nations, the High Ambition Coalition, support these provisions in the treaty negotiations. However, the plastics and petrochemical industries

---

[5] See pages 34–35 in this volume.
[6] See page 42 in this volume.

as well as major petrostates, led by Saudi Arabia and Russia, oppose these provisions. Negotiations will continue in 2025.[7]

The chapter ought to be frequently invoked and cited. It is magisterial, a model expression of a method to offer empowering information for a daunting collective project. Wisely, the authors conclude echoing Pope Francis' own advocacy.

I think of this first chapter as the head of this manual; it is filled with information: a veritable executive summary of the challenges before us. The remaining chapters provide resources in the fight to advocate for the treaty and the more enduring issue of reducing plastic production and its attendant inequities. These address two different needs: first, needed ethical argumentation. Here are three essays that capture the heart of this manual. These essays move and enlighten us with frameworks for organizing the foundations of our responses. The second are four pieces that provide a roadmap, and these are the legs of the manual. They take us collectively on our way.

Ethical Foundations for Our Responses

Three ethicists make singular contributions in this work: Willis Jenkins from the University of Virginia, on religious ethics and environmental humanities, Christina G. McRorie on economic justice and moral agency, and Andrea Vicini on Catholic social teaching.

The intrepid Jenkins has long guided fellow ethicists in understanding and engaging the environment. Now Jenkins invites us to encounter our own plasticity. He begins his empowering reflection, "In early Christian thought the word 'plastic' often referred to the human being. From the Greek verb *plassō* for molding and making, emerged a word for the quality of being able to be molded: *plastikos*—the quality of being formable by the intent of another." He adds: "from the New Testament into the

---

[7] See pages 45–46 in this volume.

nineteenth century, a primary referent for 'plastic' in Christian theology was the human interior, transformable before the creativity of God."[8]

Jenkins notes that today plastic is the name of "a scourge, a pervasive light that itself seems to be altering lifeworlds" and wonders whether "plastic will become the signature geological evidence of an epoch of irresponsible anthropogenic influence: the plasticene."[9] This radical shift from something of promise to now an existential threat prompts us to stay with the original meaning of the word. Jenkins retrieves this original notion of plastic wherein we are "molded by God into responsibility for all one's relations."[10] He encourages us to "become more plastic."[11]

He also suggests that by becoming more plastic, we might confront our own colonial inclinations that underlie the distribution of the chaos of plastic and the injustices that they promote. He notes that by confronting that mentality, we might not only make ourselves more plastic to address our challenges, but we also might be able to undo the belief that plastic pollution is inevitably to become worse. Indeed, by recognizing how historically problematic we were in the past, we might learn how to unravel the scourge of the present. He concludes with five tactics, the last being to recognize the agential "rights of rivers and oceans."[12]

Like Jenkins, McRorie focuses on the fact that "it seems undeniable now that the destructive consequences of our overuse of plastics are many, and that these are distributed unequally, with the heaviest burdens borne by those with least power and privilege."[13] Still, like Jenkins, McRorie focuses on human agency to respond to this crisis and looks on the challenge "as an economic question, seen in light of the principle of the preferential option for the poor."[14] Again, like Jenkins, McRorie insists

---

[8] See page 67 in this volume.
[9] See page 67 in this volume.
[10] See page 69 in this volume.
[11] See page 69 in this volume.
[12] See page 80 in this volume.
[13] See pages 84–85 in this volume.
[14] See page 83 in this volume.

that to get away from our colonial mentality then, we need to find ways to "include empowering *their* agency. This keeps this principle from becoming paternalistic and mere charity: to truly have an enduring commitment to the dignity of the most vulnerable means acting to empower them as agents in their own lives and following their lead when it comes to solving problems that affect them."[15]

McRorie recognizes that some economists, indeed, want to face the global reality that top-down decisions by those who manage market incentives are necessary and that we should work for laws that accomplish this. But she also sees the present predicament as at once a challenge and yet an invitation to a transformative and more just economics. She raises up Elinor Ostrom's Nobel-prize winning work on how local communities governed "communal resources such as fisheries and forests *without* having these managed by a centralized state authority."[16]

Like Olstrom, McRorie prompts us "not to think that the only fix for social dilemmas is to have the state itself restrict self-interested behavior in markets but to also focus on institutions" that 'bring out the best in humans.'"[17] With that prompt in mind, McRorie highlights other ways before and beyond the state that communities can exercise and practice through a true economically just moral agency. In her argument, it seems to me, she sees the present predicament as a kenotic moment to understand and construct more local, transparent, and equitable economic structures that fit the contours of local societies.

As McRorie invokes the option for the poor as an indispensable hermeneutical key for morally just local and national economies, Andrea Vicini invites a full embrace of the Catholic social justice tradition. In his refreshing essay, Vicini raises up the necessary virtue of social trust as indispensable for any reforms. In advancing three necessary responsive strategies, he first highlights the need to pair personal and social agency by

---

[15] See page 84 in this volume.
[16] See page 88 in this volume.
[17] See page 89 in this volume.

highlighting the virtues and the practices of prudence, justice, and solidarity. Echoing McRorie's concerns on agency, Vicini proffers virtues that not only can connect and make possible more responsible social agency but also inflame a social trust that is desperately needed today.

Vicini then insists on a vigilance for keeping in tension the political and the economic, echoing the core of McRorie's thesis. He concludes by interfacing the technological with the critical. Just as McRorie warns us against a belief that the state alone can change plastic pollution, so too Vicini warns us that "to presume that technology is *the* only solution and that technological fixes alone can respond to what affects human beings and the planet betrays what Pope Francis has called the 'technocratic paradigm.'"[18] He proposes that we "articulate a critical assessment of technological developments and strengthen our social awareness and critical engagements, which might imply promoting environmentally sustainable alternatives and embracing forms of resistance to unquestioned uses of plastic products."[19] He concludes arguing that "education and formation are integral to the ongoing task of empowering moral agents and fostering needed structural transformations and changes."[20] I would add that this collection of essays is precisely an instrument for promoting that education and formation.

Pathways Forward

With the conference report and three ethics essays as foundations for a response, we now turn to the four final essays that prompt us on our pathways to personally and collectively respond to the crisis of plastics pollution.

First, Margaret Spring, JD, a member of the Minderoo-Monaco Commission on Plastics and Human Health, and a co-author of its 2023

---

[18] See page 105 in this volume.
[19] See page 106 in this volume.
[20] See page 107 in this volume.

report, and Cindy Matuch, a Science-Policy Fellow, who works with Spring at the Monterey Bay Aquarium, provide a historical narrative of the advancement of the global treaty. They trace the five meetings starting with the first in Punta del Este Uruguay in March 2022, when "over 175 countries approved UNEA Resolution 5/14, which called for the development of an international legally-binding agreement to tackle plastic pollution, including in the marine environment."[21] We learn that "the specific mandate was to develop an instrument, based on a comprehensive approach that addresses the full life cycle of plastic and that would include both binding and voluntary approaches."[22]

Subsequent meetings in France, Kenya, and Canada "continued consideration of the key elements that would form part of a treaty text."[23] Spring and Matuch explain the convergences and divergences in the pursuit of the treaty. The fifth meeting, held in Busan, Republic of Korea, from November 25–December 1, 2024, "was intended to be the final round of negotiations. However, while it brought several advancements, the meeting ultimately concluded without agreement on a final treaty text. Delegates agreed to reconvene in 2025 for a subsequent session."[24]

The authors "saw both significant progress and persistent challenges, signaling cautious optimism about the treaty's future."[25] Noting "the increased ambition displayed by a growing number of member states," they reported that:

> Over one hundred countries expressed support for the text's proposals to reduce the production of primary plastic polymers in alignment with global targets. Additionally, ninety-four countries backed a declaration calling for legally-binding obligations to phase out the most harmful plastic products and chemicals of concern. Eighty-five members

---

[21] See page 110 in this volume.
[22] See page 110 in this volume.
[23] See page 112 in this volume.
[24] See page 113 in this volume.
[25] See page 114 in this volume.

supported a declaration referencing four key measures that would form part of an ambitious instrument.[26]

With the expectation of a treaty in 2025, they see "that it may be two, three, or more, years between finalization of the initial treaty text and entry into force."[27]

The Reverend Mitchell C. Hescox, President Emeritus of the Evangelical Environmental Network, provides a "moral roadmap for ending the global plastics crisis" and helpfully notes that "most attempts to mobilize Americans for a plastic-free future utilize language and value appeals that are inconsistent with conservatives' core values."[28]

He argues that the possibility of change "depends on engaging existing faith and moral frameworks."[29] He explains that "these frameworks must include children's health (both unborn and born), the potential harm to future generations, business opportunities, efficient limited government action, and hope. Solutions must also include practical and meaningful individual engagement. Sanctity (the sacredness of life) and purity (morally untainted) are the top moral values for the conservative evangelical community."[30] He adds, "meaningful communication and education in our community must focus on these two primary concerns—the best and most common messages for our community."[31]

I found most instructive that for a community that depends on wisdom from Scripture alone, the argument for tending to the environment must invoke the bible. Specifically, Hescox narrates the force of Colossians 1:16–20 (NIV):

---

[26] See page 114 in this volume.
[27] See page 118 in this volume.
[28] See page 122 in this volume.
[29] See page 127 in this volume.
[30] See page 127 in this volume.
[31] See pages 127–128 in this volume.

> For in him all things were created: things in heaven and on earth, visible and invisible, whether thrones or powers or rulers or authorities; all things have been created through him and for him. He is before all things, and in him all things hold together. And he is the head of the body, the church; he is the beginning and the firstborn from among the dead, so that in everything he might have the supremacy. For God was pleased to have all his fullness dwell in him, and through him to reconcile to himself all things, whether things on earth or things in heaven, by making peace through his blood, shed on the cross.

From this text, he argues that "Christians are not the owners of the Earth. The Earth, God's creation, was formed by and for God, by and for Jesus. Unfortunately, too many Christians, especially evangelicals, do not understand the imperative to 'work it and take care of it [the Earth].'"[32] Of course, the command to care for the Earth is from Genesis 2:15, God's very first instruction to the human, the first task humanity given by God.

Hescox concludes noting again that the preeminent concern of conveying environmental threat by stressing its impact on our children.

The volume concludes with three religious salutations and a message from the Prince of Monaco to commend us on these pathways. From Rabbi Leonid Feldman, we are called to repairing our world—Tikkun Olam—stressing our responsibility to work towards healing the environment and be good stewards of God's creation. From His All-Holiness Ecumenical Patriarch Bartholomew, we are invited "to approach our world as something invaluable and spiritual—that is to say, as something that we received as a gift from above and from our ancestors."[33] But then he adds not only should we honor the world as gift, but we should treat it with thanksgiving as we hand it "down to our children in love—then we will invariably respect it as something far greater than us and our interests."[34] From the Dalai Lama, we are exhorted to a "genuine sense of

---

[32] See page 133 in this volume.
[33] See page 142 in this volume.
[34] See page 142 in this volume.

universal responsibility."[35] Finally, from the Prince of Monaco, we are invited to join his commitment and engagement to address "the crucial issue of plastic pollution."[36]

In short, Vicini, Landrigan, and Bullock provide in this collection a true handbook for collectively facing and moving beyond the enormous threat of global plastic pollution. It could not come at a more urgent time in the history of humanity and the world.

James F. Keenan, SJ, is Vice Provost for Global Engagement, Canisius Professor in the Theology Department, and Director of the Jesuit Institute, at Boston College, and previously held the Gasson Chair and then the Founders Professorship in Theology. He earned his doctorate from the Pontifical Gregorian University in Rome and taught at Fordham University and at the Weston Jesuit School of Theology. He was Visiting Professor at Dharmaram Vidya Kshetram (Bangalore, India), the Pontifical Gregorian University (Rome, Italy), and Ateneo de Manila University (Philippines). He has authored and edited over a dozen of books and hundreds of articles and book chapters, and founded and directed the Moral Traditions Series of volumes in theological ethics published by Georgetown University Press. Globally, he was the founder and co-chair of the network Catholic Theological Ethics in the World Church and contributed to organize regional and global conferences and two book series. Member of numerous boards, he was also consultor of the US Conference of Catholic Bishops for the revision of the *Ethical and Religious Directives for Catholic Health Care Services* and the New York State Transplant Council, and was Group Leader of the Surgeon General's Task Force on Responsible Sexual Conduct.

---

[35] See page 144 in this volume.
[36] See page 147 in this volume.

www.ingramcontent.com/pod-product-compliance
Lightning Source LLC
Chambersburg PA
CBHW062047220426
43662CB00010B/1687